MICROCOMPUTER Software Design

HOW TO DEVELOP COMPLEX APPLICATION PROGRAMS

SALLY CAMPBELL

A SPECTRUM BOOK

PRENTICE-HALL INC. Englewood Cliffs, New Jersey 07632

Library of Congress Cataloging in Publication Data

Campbell, Sally.
   Microcomputer software design.

  "A Spectrum Book."
  Bibliography: p.
  Includes Index.
  1. Microcomputers—Programming. 2. System design.
I. Title.
QA76.6.C345 1983   001.64′25   83-8243
ISBN 0-13-580639-9
ISBN 0-13-580621-6 (pbk.)

This book is available at a special price when ordered in
bulk quantities. Contact Prentice-Hall, Inc., General
Publishing Division, Special Sales, Englewood Cliffs, N.J. 07632

© 1984 by Prentice-Hall, Inc., Englewood Cliffs, New Jersey 07632.
All rights reserved. No part of this book may be reproduced in any form
or by any means without permission in writing from the publisher.
A SPECTRUM BOOK. Printed in the United States of America.

1 2 3 4 5 6 7 8 9 10

To my junior and senior high school English teachers:

Robert G. Simmons
Enid Treffinger
Eleanor Stewart
Malcolm Moore

ISBN 0-13-580621-6 {PBK.}

ISBN 0-13-580639-9

Production/editorial supervision and interior design
  by Cyndy Lyle Rymer
Manufacturing buyer: Cathie Lenard
Cover and jacket design © 1984 by Jeannette Jacobs

Prentice-Hall International, Inc., London
Prentice-Hall of Australia Pty. Limited, Sydney
Prentice-Hall Canada Inc., Toronto
Prentice-Hall of India Private Limited, New Delhi
Prentice-Hall of Japan, Inc., Tokyo
Prentice-Hall of Southeast Asia Pte. Ltd., Singapore
Whitehall Books Limited, Wellington, New Zealand
Editora Prentice-Hall do Brasil Ltda., Rio de Janeiro

Contents

GETTING STARTED

1 / Introduction, *3*
A WORD ABOUT WORDS, 5   HARDWARE BASICS, 7
COMPUTER PROGRAMS, 17
THE PROGRAM DEVELOPMENT CYCLE, 20

2 / Problem Definition, *23*
DEFINING A PROBLEM DEFINITION, 25
START WITH A "FUZZY", 27
THE COMPLETE PROBLEM DEFINITION, 36   SUMMARY, 39

FUNCTIONAL DESIGN

3 / Modular Program Design, *45*
ELEMENTS OF THE STRUCTURE DIAGRAM, 47
PAYROLL EXAMPLE, 56   ADVANCED TECHNIQUES, 61
REVIEW OF STRUCTURE DIAGRAM DEVELOPMENT, 64
SUMMARY, 66

4 / HIPOs, *68*
THE HIPO PACKAGE, 69   ABOUT IPO DIAGRAMS, 77
EXTENDED DESCRIPTIONS, 83   MORE IPOs, 85   SUMMARY, 91

DETAILED DESIGN

5 / Decision Tables, *97*

CONTENT AND CONSTRUCTION, 99
ENCHANTING DECISION TABLES, 106   SUMMARY, 110

6 / Flowcharting, *112*

SYMBOLOGY, 114   CONCLUSION, 133

7 / Pseudocode, *135*

RETURN TO WORDS, 136   SUMMARY, 146

8 / Data Definitions, *148*

DATA FILE ACCESS METHODS, 158   FILE SIZES, 164

QUALITY ASSURANCE

9 / Error Detection, *169*

ERROR DETECTION METHODS, 173   SUMMARY, 181

10 / Testing, *183*

OVERVIEW OF TESTING, 186
PLANNING FOR TESTING, 188
PREPARING FOR TESTING, 191
PERFORMING TESTING, 194

CONCLUSION

11 / Loose Ends and Last Words, *199*

DOCUMENTATION, 200   ATTITUDES, 205
YOUR "OTHER" LIFE, 206   LEARNING MORE, 208

Appendices, 209

APPENDIX A: COMPARISON OF
COMMON PROGRAMMING LANGUAGES, 210
APPENDIX B: ADDITIONAL ACTION VERBS, 211
APPENDIX C: ANSI STANDARD SYSTEM
AND PROGRAM FLOWCHARTING SYMBOLS, 212

Glossary, 213

Bibliography, 225

Preface

Microcomputers are here to stay, and they seem to be everywhere. I believe anyone can learn how to write simple programs for microcomputers. However, efficient and effective development of complex programs requires the discipline of design tools and techniques involved in the program development cycle.

Historically, this knowledge has been harbored by computer professionals after months of on-the-job training or independent study. Although volumes have been written more recently, there seems to be no central source of information on program design and development that can be understood by people outside the profession.

This book captures the essence of the program development cycle by presenting a complete set of design tools and techniques in the order they are typically applied. Its focus is on the design of a microcomputer program, regardless of the programming language that may be used. From the inception of an idea for a program through testing of the final product, each chapter concentrates on how and why each tool and technique is used. In many cases, the thought processes required to affect an efficient design are carefully explained.

The tools and techniques presented include the development of a sound problem definition, development of structure diagrams, creation of an HIPO package, creation and simplification of decision tables, design and use of basic data structures, creation of legible flowcharts, generation and use of pseudocode, and assurance of program quality through a variety of error-detection methods.

Because this book is intended for non-computer people, each of the design tools is described in common terms. Each of the tools and techniques could be explored in much greater detail. However, the intent of this book is to convey a general working knowledge that can be applied to a program development project. The explanation of the tools includes both content and construct so the reader will understand what the particular tool accomplishes as well as the steps involved in its creation. Summary lists of development steps and questions are provided where applicable. Continuity among the discrete design tools is achieved by developing design of a single program throughout the book.

The book takes a human approach to program design while remaining technically sound. Some of the tools are illustrated first with non-computer examples before the rigors of development are applied to the same problem(s). Also, the chapters dealing with error detection stress the human factors of ego involvement, and the last chapter explores the hazards of becoming microcomputer- or programming-addicted. Finally, a comprehensive glossary of terms used in the book is included for quick reference.

The sequential structure of this book lends itself nicely to a concurrent development of a program project. I chose a simplified payroll system for the example used throughout the book because most people understand the basics of creating paychecks and the importance of accuracy in producing a payroll. (All names and numbers are strictly fictitious.) At times some examples may appear tedious and unnecessary. This was unavoidable considering my intent not to overwhelm the reader with detail. I suggest that as each chapter is read, the new tool or technique should be applied to an actual problem. This ensures that a sound working knowledge of the material will be obtained before the next topic is explored.

ACKNOWLEDGMENTS

I have written this book on the urging of my students and colleagues. Without many people, however, I would never have been equipped with the knowledge or professional experience to have had this opportunity. I extend my special thanks to:

- My mom and dad for their love and encouragement to believe in myself and use the gifts I possess.
- My brother Keith for having shared with me his enthusiasm for computers since 1963.
- My brother Dick for having a wonderful family through which I can vicariously indulge my maternal instincts.
- The patient in the hospital where I worked as a lab assistant for arranging my first programming job interview.
- My former colleagues for having taught me the right way to develop programs.
- My friend and unbiased critic Arabrab Retluoc Kciredorb (Barbara Coulter Broderick) for typing, editing, and improving this work, and for amusing me with her ability to talk backwards.
- My diligent helpers and colleagues at Pepperdine for their legwork and compassion.
- And especially my friend and mentor Karl Albrecht, for everything.

Sally Campbell is an administrative data processing manager in charge of software systems at Pepperdine University, Malibu, California. She has designed and developed microcomputer software, and has served as a consultant, lecturer, and instructor on microcomputer management use and program development.

GETTING STARTED

1

Introduction

1

Do you have a great idea for a computer program? Do you want to ensure that it will perform as you imagine it will? Do you think you'll ever want to make the program more powerful? Designing a computer program is very similar to designing a building. If the building is not architecturally sound with a solid foundation, it could collapse into a pile of rubble. Similarly, if a computer program is not well-designed, it may not meet your expectations and could cease to function, or *crash,* as computer people say. To make matters even more difficult, adding on to a poorly designed program may be as time-consuming and expensive as rebuilding a collapsed building.

Each of you is about to begin a construction process known as microcomputer program design. Although this book will provide you with guidelines or blueprints, it is up to you to use these tools to complete your project. You will have to accomplish many small steps before you build your program design. In doing so, you will explore the full gamut of the program design process. First, you'll begin with developing a sound problem definition. This is the first step toward building the program's framework. Next, you'll expand on this definition and decide what shape your project will take, how you anticipate fitting all of your program features together, and what tools will be most helpful in your task. Finally, you will learn which techniques you can use to ensure that your program design is sound.

As with any construction project, you will need building supplies and an understanding of the basic terminology of the profession. This introductory chapter will provide you with this background. It will introduce you to common microcomputer terminology, and explain terminology related to programming. Also, this chapter will briefly explore the program development cycle.

A WORD ABOUT WORDS

Before you begin learning computer terminology, it is best for you to understand a few anomalies about the computing field's jargon. Perhaps the most frustrating fact about the terminology is that there are often several words with the same meaning, just as there are often words that take on a variety of meanings. This can be very frustrating for the novice who insists on very specific language. For example, the word *processor* may refer to a part of the computer or to part of a structure diagram. Another word having two meanings is *format,* which may refer to the physical appearance of a report or to the special characters used with numbers to indicate dollar amounts. There are many more examples. Simply remember that whenever you have doubts about the meaning of a particular word, you can look it up in the Glossary.

Computer terminology has evolved in conjunction with the rapid advances of computer technology, a process that has taken place over the past three decades. These rapid technological advances have yielded new words and phrases. The field has been characterized as highly competitive, with computer manufacturers such as IBM, Sperry, and Burroughs in the large-scale, or mainframe, environment, and Apple, Tandy, and Commodore in the very small-scale, or micro, environment. Each manufacturer has had to sell its products to the consumer, and one way of doing this has been to conjure up different names to describe essentially the same thing.

In some cases, the computer terminology you encounter may seem frivolous or trite. Well, it is true that "computer types" have had some fun coining terms. For example, a *bit* is either a zero or a one; nothing more and nothing less. This term actually is an acronym for *b*inary dig*it.* A *byte* (pronounced bite) consists of eight bits. Someone thought it would be fun to call four bits a *nibble,* and so they are. The fact that some words seem silly, however, doesn't render them any less useful. Try to enjoy the humor in the words, and think of this built-in humor as one way of spicing up an otherwise dull subject.

Acronyms in the computer field also can be quite confusing. For example, the context surrounding the use of the letters *CPM* must be known in order to understand the meaning of the letters. In this example, if one is speaking of a programming project management tool, he or she is referring to the *critical path method.* However, if one is talking about a program that controls the activity of a microcomputer, he or she is referring to the *CP/M* operating system.

There are literally thousands of these words and acronyms that have specific meanings in the computer field. New terms will be introduced throughout the book as new tools and techniques are explained. The next section will be devoted to explaining some very basic terms of the computer field. If you have already taken an introduction to data processing course, you may wish to skip this section.* However, it may be wise to quickly read through it to ensure that you have the same operative definition of the terms used throughout the book.

Fundamental Terminology

Computer *systems* consist of two basic components: hardware and software. Both the hardware and software must be operating properly for the system to be *up*—functioning and available for use. If something as simple as a power outage or as complex as a critical electrical component failure occurs, the computer system will no longer function. When the system is not up, it is said to be *down*.

The *hardware* of the computer system comprises the electrical parts, or the physical components of the system. Computers come in all shapes and sizes, ranging from the very large and powerful to the very small but remarkably powerful. The gradations in size are called *large-scale* computers, *medium-scale* computers, *minicomputers,* and *microcomputers.*

Computer *programs* are the *software* that make a computer do what its human operators tell it to do. Software is written in a *programming language* that can ultimately be understood by the computer. Programs are written to perform certain functions or solve specific problems. When the program is run or *executed,* the computer follows the programmed instructions.

Typically, the program takes in *data* in the form of letters *(alpha characters),* numbers *(numeric characters), special characters,* or any combination of these. This recognition by the program of data outside the program is called *input.* The data are, figuratively, *put into* the computer. The program will then *process* the input data

---

*If you have not taken an introductory course but want a general understanding of computers, I recommend you read *Computer Consciousness: Surviving the Automated 80s,* by H. Dominic Covvey and Neil Harding (Addison-Wesley Publishing Co. Inc.). It is a short, humorous, and quite thorough introduction that doesn't belabor the history of computers.

by manipulating them in some fashion. This processing may involve alphabetizing *(sorting)*, performing mathematical calculations *(calculating)*, or saving *(storing)* the data for future processing.

Eventually, the results of the processing will be needed outside the computer. In transferring these data to another medium, the data are *output* from the computer. The processes of input and output are frequently referred to as *I/O,* and pronounced "eye-oh."

If a program does not input, process, or output the data correctly, it is said to have a *bug* or problem. Some bugs are worse than others. A bug resulting in an incorrect answer is typically not as serious as a bug causing the program to *crash* (go from an up state to a down state). Trying to locate the bug in a program is called *debugging.* (Sometimes you may wish the term was exterminating! A can of insecticide may seem more effective for eradicating those elusive bugs!)

HARDWARE BASICS

Every computer system that can execute programs consists of a main computer and other devices called *peripherals*. Peripherals are attached to the computer to facilitate input and output of data. The microcomputer contains two functional components, *memory* and the *processor*. Memory in microcomputers is divided into two general categories: read only memory (ROM) and random access memory (RAM). Read Only Memory is a portion of the microcomputer that has computer instructions permanently placed at specific locations. This area always contains the same information and cannot be replaced by a program. Random Access Memory is where programs must reside in order to be interpreted and executed by the computer. Typically, your program will be able to use only a portion of a microcomputer's RAM. This is called address space. The actual amount of it depends on the machine and its operating system. Whatever the actual usable amount of RAM available, your entire program must be in RAM in order to be executed.

The processor is the physical portion of the computer that performs computer instructions (in binary). The actual method by which this occurs depends on the physical design or *architecture* of the microcomputer. The size of a computer is determined by the number of bytes contained in its memory. An 8,000-byte machine has 8,000 (or 8K) bytes of RAM area in the computer.* Similarly, a 64K machine has 64,000 bytes of RAM. Where additional RAM is available for a computer, the vast majority of it is available for program usage.

The power of a computer is determined by the number of bits the computer uses to form its electronic instructions. The technical explanation for this is somewhat complex. It will suffice for you to understand that a 16-bit machine is far more powerful than an 8-bit machine.

A few years ago, computers were physically quite large. Generally, the larger the computer, the more powerful it was. However, this trend was practically reversed with the invention of the silicon chip. This small component, about the size of your thumbnail, contains very tiny electronic circuitry between very thin layers of a glass-like substance. The electricity enters and leaves the chip through pins that make the chip look something like a centipede.

One of these chips now represents the amount of main memory that used to be contained in a computer roughly the size of a large refrigerator. These chips have allowed computers to decrease in size while increasing in power. As smaller and more powerful computers were developed, they became known as minicomputers. As they became even smaller, the term *microcomputer* was coined. Currently, it is agreed among professionals that there is little or no difference between a mini- and a microcomputer. Microcomputers have the capability of performing functions which only a few years ago could be performed solely on much larger computers. In fact, specialized chips containing the computer processor and a few memory chips can now perform the same functions faster than old computers the size of large dump trucks.

The components of a microcomputer, those internal organs that dictate the various capabilities of a particular computer, are called *printed-circuit boards,* or simply *boards.* Boards are rather thin pieces of insulated material with thin layers of metal coating. These thin, squiggly lines of metal carry electricity to the other electrical components such as chips, which are plugged into the boards by their pins. The combinations of the components allow the computer to perform various functions. For example, one board may allow your program to send its output to a printer, whereas another will allow your program to interact with a different program in a second micro-

---

*These numbers are rounded. They actually represent multiples of 2^{10} or 1,024.

FIGURE 1.1.
MSC 8001 Single-Board Microcomputer
(Courtesy of Monolithic Systems Corporation).

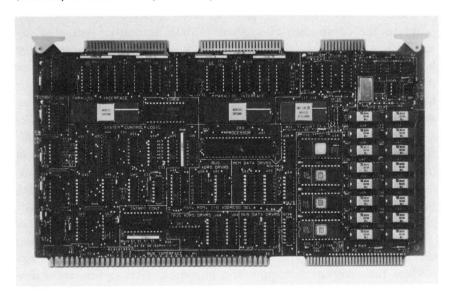

computer. Figure 1-1 shows a 12" × 6.75" printed-circuit board that comprises an 8K memory, 8-bit processor microcomputer.

Just as an automobile is built around a central chassis, a microcomputer is assembled around a *motherboard.* The motherboard provides a certain number of slots that can be filled with boards to provide the interface for peripheral equipment or languages. Since the motherboard itself cannot be expanded, the number of slots available in the motherboard limits the capabilities of the microcomputer.

Peripheral equipment refers to all of the components that make up an integrated computer system. Examples of common peripheral equipment are display units, keyboards, auxiliary storage units, and printers. Less frequently used peripherals include voice or music synthesizers, plotters, and joysticks.

A *display unit* is an apparatus on which the results of manual entry to the computer or the results of a program can be seen. For some systems, it is the only way the computer can "talk" to an individual. The display may be as simple as a series of lights on the computer, or as complex as a three dimensional drawing on a television screen referred to as a CRT (cathode ray tube). Most typically, a display unit is a CRT with words drawn or displayed on its screen. Most people have been introduced to this type of device in places such as airports, where television-like CRTs are used to display airline departures and arrivals.

Most display units are used to show a person what has been input to the computer. This input of data normally takes place by typing on a *keyboard*. This keyboard is usually very similar to the keys on a typewriter. Some keyboards also include a numeric key pad similar to an adding machine. These keys are desirable if the user has a need to enter large quantities of numeric data. Whenever information is entered into the computer via a keyboard, it is *keyed* in.

Often, the CRT and keyboard are referred to as a *display unit*. Keyboards can be permanently and firmly attached to the CRT, or may be attached with a wire which allows the user to move the keyboard to a comfortable working position. Figure 1-2 shows a video display unit with a detached keyboard. The light colored keys on the right-hand side of the keyboard make up the unit's numeric key pad.

Auxiliary storage is a third type of peripheral equipment that can be added to a computer system. Usually, only one program can occupy the computer's memory at one time. Thus, whenever a new program is entered, the previous program is lost and must be reen-

FIGURE 1-2. Personal Computer with Video Display Unit, Detachable Keyboard, and Dual Floppy Disk Drives (Courtesy of NEC Information Systems, Inc.).

FIGURE 1-3. Approximate Auxiliary Storage Medium Capacities.

STORAGE MEDIUM	MEGABYTES (MB)	K-BYTES (K)	BYTES
Cassette Tape	.1 — .3	100 — 300	100,000 — 300,000
5¼" Floppy Diskette	.07 — .28	70 — 280	70,000 — 280,000
8" Floppy Diskette	.25 — 1.0	250 — 1,000	250,000 — 1,000,000
5½" Winchester Disk	5 — 10	5,000 — 10,000	5,000,000 — 10,000,000
8" Winchester Disk	10 — 20	10,000 — 20,000	10,000,000 — 20,000,000

tered to be executed. A programmer usually does not want to key in a program every time it is to be run, and there are times when it will be desirable to store the data the program uses. Auxiliary storage allows the user to store the program and program data until it is needed. Storage may be in the form of a *cassette tape,* similar to that used for recording music, or a *floppy diskette,* a thin and flexible disk resembling a small record. A hard *disk,* another form of storage, is much larger than a floppy diskette, and it stores much more data. Some hard disks are called *Winchester disks* because of their design technology. Figure 1-3 illustrates the amount of storage capacity that may be available with each type of storage medium. The amount of storage available is referred to in terms of millions of bytes, or characters, of information. Floppy diskettes, for example, can be written on one side or two sides, and in single or double density. Floppy diskettes come in three sizes, 3½-inch, 5¼-inch and 8-inch, and in combinations of single side, double side, single density and double density. Figure 1-4 compares the storage available on the different types of floppies.*

The information is stored on and retrieved from the floppy or hard disk through a peripheral unit called a floppy or hard-disk *drive.* The disk drive contains the electrical components necessary to spin the disk past the magnetic sensors, which detect the zeros and ones

---

*3½-inch floppies have not been standardized. To date, storage capacities range from 164K bytes to 328K bytes.

FIGURE 1-4. Floppy Diskette Storage Capacity (in thousands of bytes).

5¼"	SINGLE DENSITY	DOUBLE DENSITY
Single Side	70	140
Double Side	140	280

8"	SINGLE DENSITY	DOUBLE DENSITY
Single Side	250	500
Double Side	500	1,000

comprising the information stored. Figure 1-5 shows the components of a Winchester (hard) disk drive. The platters that look like phonograph records are the hard disks on which the information is stored. The metal fingers reaching between the platters hold the magnetic sensors, or *heads*.

FIGURE 1.5. 8-inch Winchester Disk Drive (Courtesy of NEC Information Systems, Inc.).

The amount of storage you may require generally is a function of your experience level. As you become more comfortable with computers and their uses, you will usually think of new ways to tap this important resource. If a microcomputer is being used for text manipulation—for example, writing term papers—a single diskette may not be adequate for data storage. For the programmer who works with a very limited number of programs, however, a single diskette may be all that is required.

One of the first pieces of peripheral equipment typically added to a microcomputer system is a printer. A printer (see Figure 1-6) allows information from a program to be output on to paper so that it can be removed from the computer and kept in readable form. This is called producing *hard copy*. Printers come in a variety of shapes and sizes, with a wide range of costs, but the major differences lie in the quality of the printed characters and the speed at which printers operate. There are two basic types of printers currently available. The first is called a *dot-matrix* printer. The dot-matrix printer forms letters by configuring a grid of dots (see Figure 1-7). The quality of the printed character depends on the number of dots available for each character. The more dots there are, the closer together they will be, and the better quality the character. Figure 1-8 shows samples of dot matrix printing. The size of the characters is measured in characters per inch, or cpi.

A second type of printer is a *letter-quality* printer. These printers contain preset metal or plastic figures, such as those on a type-

FIGURE 1-6. Peripheral Printer
(Courtesy of Texas Instruments, Inc.).

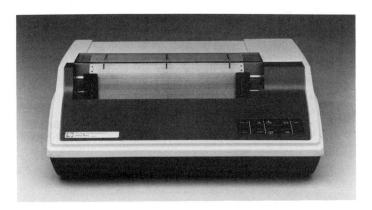

FIGURE 1-7. Example of a Dot Matrix Letter.

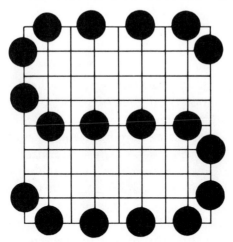

FIGURE 1-8. 9-Pin Dot Matrix-Printing Samples (Courtesy of EPSON America, Inc.).

10 CPI
THIS IS NORMAL.
THIS IS NORMAL,ITALICS.
THIS IS NORMAL,DOUBLESTRIKE.
THIS IS NORMAL,DOUBLESTRIKE,ITALICS.
THIS IS NORMAL,EMPHASIZED,DOUBLESTRIKE.
THIS IS NORMAL,EMPHASIZED,DOUBLESTRIKE,ITALICS.
THIS IS SUPERSCRIPT.
THIS IS SUPERSCRIPT,ITALICS.

5 CPI
THIS IS DOUBLEWIDTH.
THIS IS DOUBLEWIDTH,ITALICS.
THIS IS DOUBLEWIDTH,EMPHASIZED.
THIS IS DOUBLEWIDTH,EMPHASIZED, ITALICS.
THIS IS DOUBLEWIDTH,EMPHASIZED, DOUBLESTRIKE.
THIS IS DOUBLEWIDTH,EMPHASIZED, DOUBLESTRIKE,ITALICS.

8.58 CPI
THIS IS CONDENSED,DOUBLEWIDTH.
THIS IS CONDENSED,DOUBLEWIDTH,ITALICS.
THIS IS CONDENSED,DOUBLEWIDTH,DOUBLESTRIKE.
THIS IS CONDENSED,DOUBLEWIDTH,DOUBLESTRIKE,ITALICS.

17.16 CPI
THIS IS CONDENSED.
THIS IS CONDENSED,ITALICS.
THIS IS CONDENSED,DOUBLESTRIKE.
THIS IS CONDENSED,DOUBLESTRIKE,ITALICS.
THIS IS CONDENSED,SUPERSCRIPT.
THIS IS CONDENSED,SUPERSCRIPT,ITALICS.

FIGURE 1-9. Thimbles Used on Letter Quality Printers (Courtesy of NEC Information Systems, Inc.).

writer, which strike the paper to form the character. Figure 1-9 shows the thimbles used on some letter-quality printers.

Now you have an idea of what components can be brought together in a computer system. A computer with a complement of peripheral equipment is known as a *configuration*. Figure 1-10 shows a configuration consisting of a display unit with detachable keyboard, a printer, and the computer, including an 8-inch floppy disk and a 5¼-inch Winchester disk.

FIGURE 1-10. Personal Computer Configuration (Courtesy of Texas Instruments, Inc.).

Computer systems need not be bulky and difficult to transport. Some microcomputers, such as that shown in Figure 1-11, are only the size of a briefcase, and contain a detachable keyboard with a numeric key pad, a video display unit, and two 5¼-inch floppy disk drives. If hardcopy output is desired, this microcomputer can accommodate a printer.

The number of peripherals which can be attached to your microcomputer is determined by the number of slots in its motherboard and the specific electronic characteristics of each slot. (The technological reasons for this would require too much discussion to be appropriate for this book.)

It may be possible for you to add some less-common peripherals, such as *synthesizers*, to your system to enhance the computer's configuration. Synthesizers can be programmed to make audible sounds. Some are capable of making music, while others can simulate human speech. Music synthesizers and a graphic display unit (upon which pictures can be drawn) are the tools used in creating some animated cartoons, such as those used in advertising. Color graphics and sound are also combined in video games. In order to control some of the animated figures, the computer is configured

FIGURE 1-11. Portable 64K Microcomputer
(Courtesy of Osborne Computer Corporation).

with a *joystick*. Considering the joystick's association with computer games, and the endless hours spent by video game fans attempting to master these games, the peripheral is aptly named! You should now be familiar with the major hardware components utilized in computer systems, but what can be done with this hardware? Without a computer program, nothing. The next section of this chapter concerns computer programs.

COMPUTER PROGRAMS

One of the best analogies for understanding the difference between the microcomputer and the program is that of an airplane and its pilot. Quite literally, the airplane will not go anywhere without a pilot. The pilot mans the controls, steers the plane, and makes the critical decisions for its operation. The airplane, on the other hand, merely reacts to the actions of the pilot. Computer programs act in a way similar to the pilot. The programs man the computer's controls, direct the manipulation of data, and tell the hardware what to do and when to do it.

A computer does not respond to the same sort of directions that would be given by a pilot. A computer is an electronic device that understands only electrical impulses. Because computer programs are written by human beings, they must be written in special languages that can be translated into these electrical impulses. Each computer *language*—and there are many of them—has its own particular characteristics. When electronic computers were first developed, languages were quite cryptic and difficult for the programmer to master. Today, however, languages have been developed that are far more intelligible to human beings and closely resemble the English language.

A program is required whenever a computer is to perform any function at all. Therefore, programs are written for a variety of reasons, and they come in all shapes and sizes. There are very small programs for operating consumer aids such as fuel consumption gauges in automobiles or timing regulators in microwave ovens. Large programs provide the instructions in video games designed to be used with televisions. Even larger programs are written for business and provide such *applications,* or functions, as general ledger, accounts receivable, inventory control, and payroll. On an even grander scale are programs that provide simulation training for airline pilots and space-shuttle astronauts. These *simulators* are duplicates of the real cockpits with movie screen displays that reflect how the external surroundings would appear to any control stimulus. The cockpit controls respond just as if the pilots were actually in the air, and this causes the imitated external presentation to change. In this manner, they can practice flying without ever leaving the ground.

Another type of simulation program is called a *model.* Business models allow the user to set up certain parameters (such as stock market prices, inflation rates, and cost of inventory) and predict future values and activity. Business executives find models very useful in playing "What if . . . ?", helping them to make more educated, accurate business decisions. A very popular type of program used within the business environment is designed to manipulate text. These computer programs run on microcomputers usually called *word processors,* and they allow the user to type letters, memos, reports, and so on, and to correct the text as needed without retyping entire pages. With a word processor, only the errors need to be retyped—a huge time- and labor-saving tool for people working in many fields. Word processing also is designed to print the typed text the entire width of the page—from the far left column to the far right column on every line, as is the case with this page. Word processing allows the user to type letter-perfect text, perfectly aligned on both sides of the paper (called left- and right-justified), quickly and accurately.

There are also programs that coordinate the components of the computer as well as the programs designed to run on that computer. These are known as *operating systems.* Operating systems, which are provided by the computer manufacturer, are designed to coordinate the activities of the hardware and software. They provide the program with access to peripheral equipment, such as diskettes or display units. Only those applications written in languages recognized by the operating system can be run on a particular computer. For example, a program written for an Apple computer cannot be run on an IBM Personal Computer without another program to act as an interface. This program would allow the IBM computer's operating system to "pretend" to be an Apple, thereby accepting the Apple program. The converse is also true. In many cases, even when both computers are equipped with similar operating systems, it is quite possible that they will not be compatible because there may be many versions of the same system or programming language. This slight difference is called a *dialect* of the language.

Computer Languages

Before a programmer can communicate with a computer, it is necessary to learn a programming language. Computers do not understand English. Instead, they understand only electrical impulses. These impulses are configured in the form of zeros and ones. The combinations of zeros and ones form instructions to the computer, such as add, load, and write. Until fairly recently, programmers were forced to provide the computer with sets of zeros and ones—they had to communicate with the computer in its own language. This proved to be very tedious, and not always accurate. It was quite easy to misplace a zero with a one, for instance, and tell the computer to do something entirely different from what was intended. To make things simpler, computer *languages* were designed to allow the programmer to communicate on a higher level, or in a form more closely resembling the English language. These higher-level statements could then be translated into appropriate combinations of zeros and ones that would be meaningful to the computer.

This translation can be done in two ways. First, the program can be sent through a compiler and interpreted before any part of the program is executed. A *compiler* is a type of program that translates the computer language instructions of an entire program, before it is run, into the combinations of zeros and ones (*machine language* instructions). The second method is to translate higher-level language statements as they are executed, through *interpretation*. The translation takes place as each statement of the program is executed (similar to the process followed by foreign language interpreters at the United Nations). Essentially, this same line-by-line interpretation process takes place within the computer program. Of the two methods, compiling the entire program before it is executed allows the program to run much faster.

You may have read or heard of a variety of programming languages. Among them are BASIC, COBOL, FORTRAN, and Pascal. No one language is best, because each has its own particular functions and characteristics. Just as foreign languages have strengths and weaknesses, so do computer languages. (For example, did you know that in French there is no word for *weekend*? Or, that in Eskimo there are more than 30 different words to describe the color of snow?)

The COBOL language makes the printing of business reports quite simple, unlike other languages. COBOL allows the programmer to insert *formatting characters* such as a dollar sign ($) or a comma (,) in a large number. FORTRAN, however, is very clumsy for such formatting. On the other hand, FORTRAN's abbreviated instructions make mathematical calculations simple to program. The BASIC language is probably the simplest to understand initially, but it is limited in its capabilities. Pascal is not as easy to learn, but it may provide the programmer with the most flexible, general-purpose language.

Because this book is intended to teach you design techniques instead of programming techniques, very few computer-programming statements will be used in the illustrations. Once you have learned two or three programming languages, you will have the opportunity to pick your favorite and use it almost exclusively. For now, think only in terms of a program's foundation. You will learn to design a solution to a problem, not to program the solution.

Because there are so many languages available today, it would be impossible to include a complete comparison of all languages in terms of their advantages and disadvantages. Appendix A provides a quick comparison of the most common languages used on microcomputers. If you are trying to decide which language to choose, select the one that will be the easiest to use of those available for your microcomputer. Later, you will come to appreciate the general trade-offs between ease-of-use, execution speed and memory requirements inherent among the high-level and low-level languages.

THE PROGRAM DEVELOPMENT CYCLE

As you may have surmised by now, computer programs do not just happen haphazardly. Developing a program is a process that begins when you define the problem you wish to solve. The process is analogous to the design of a building. It's unwise to simply put up the timber and hope that the building will not fall down. Instead, many hours must be spent designing and testing a structure to insure that it will be able to withstand the forces of nature, and the people inhabiting it. In the same way, a computer program must be soundly designed. It is important to remember that a computer has a rather unforgiving nature. It does only what it is told to do. No more, no less. If you anticipate expanding on a program, you must plan for that expansion. It is far less expensive and time-consuming—and less frustrating—to do this during the planning stage than it is to go back and try to restructure what has already been built.

Phase One of program development is problem definition. The problem definition becomes the cornerstone of the program you construct. The foundation of that program is the design tools that will be discussed in later chapters (structure diagrams, HIPOs, decision tables, flowcharts, and pseudocode). The development cycle continues with writing the programming statements, or *coding.* This is Phase Two. The probability that the program will function as desired is increased if certain events take place during the designing and coding stages. These events, called *walkthroughs,* will also be presented later.

Phase Three, or program *testing,* is the next step in the process. Here the program is run using certain data to elicit predictable responses. The planning that goes into this testing (the goal of which is program accuracy and stability) will be explored in a later chapter.

Phase Four, usually the last phase of the program development cycle, is documenting how the program works. *Documentation* is important because it allows others to understand how the program operates. Frequently, well-written test plans and procedures are sufficient for documentation. This topic will be discussed in more depth later.

The fifth phase of the development cycle is called *enhancing* or *tweeking* a program, wherein modifications are made to slightly alter or improve the program. Once the process is complete, the program is ready to be run, and if the program is designed for someone other than the original programmer, it is ready for *delivery,* marking the end of the initial development cycle.

Most programmers are rarely satisfied with a program the first time it is written. That is not to imply that the program is not good, but as a programmer gains experience developing programs, the more likely it is that enhancements and modifications will be made. The needs and specific requirements may also change. If the programs are being written for an outside user, that user's understanding of computers and programming languages will increase with time. The level of computer literacy will be raised, and new ideas will develop. New coding techniques may also be learned with experience, and the application of these techniques may allow a programmer to redesign an old program to make it more effective.

A word of caution! Never be afraid to toss out an old program. It may seem like tossing out a favorite pair of shoes, since a great deal of sentimental value is attached to a program that has required so much energy, creativity, and time. But remember, instead, that programming is an ongoing process. The more you do it, the better you'll get—and the greater will be your chances for success.

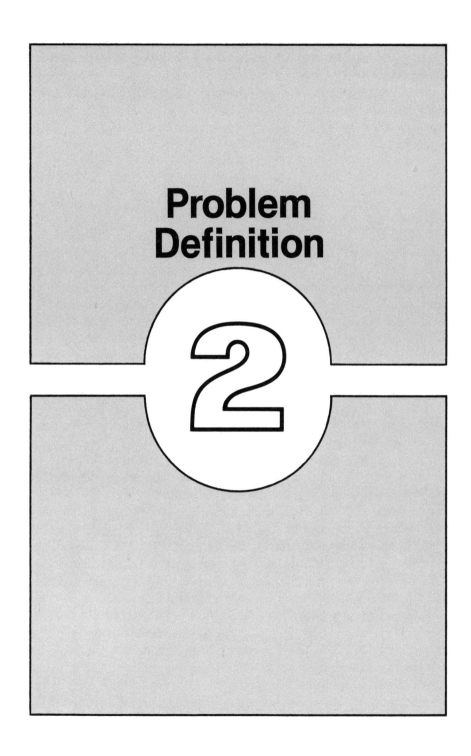

For most people faced with the task of writing, the most difficult step is simply getting started. Certainly this also pertains to writing problem definitions or project descriptions. Suddenly, with pencil in hand, one is face-to-face with the creative self, which many find difficult to confront. People frequently experience "mental blocks" when attempting to write memos, papers, articles, technical specifications, and, for this author, this book! For some reason, many writers feel compelled to write a masterpiece on the first draft—something which rarely occurs.

You too may experience anxiety when faced with developing a problem definition. On the following pages, you will be introduced to the process of defining a problem or programming project. You will be provided with a variety of questions that may help you to organize your thoughts and approach your definition methodically and logically. Although the steps involved in this process may appear simple and straightforward, each step must be performed carefully and, frequently, repeatedly.

The most important step is the first step. *Write your idea down on paper.* This is often difficult because of a natural inclination to wait until you have thought your problem through completely. However, it is difficult to examine your definition if it is not in writing. It is important to read, reread, revise, and perfect this definition before going any further. Don't worry if the project appears to be simple, silly, or much like someone else's. As long as your program will accept information from outside the computer, change that information based upon your instructions, and produce a response for external use (in other words, the program will accept input, process the data, and produce output), the problem will be complex enough for this book.

To illustrate how a simple problem can be defined, designed and developed, consider a payroll problem for a moment. This example is not aimed at designing a full payroll system. However, the design will provide the framework for easy enhancements that eventually could result in a complete system. It is important to start with a small project, one that will allow you to build confidence in your abilities, rather than a large and complex project that may only discourage you.

For this illustration, assume that a microcomputer has recently been purchased by a company, and that the basic employee information needed for calculations of paychecks is stored on diskette.

DEFINING A PROBLEM DEFINITION

Before describing the process of problem definition, it is important that you understand what type of *problem* is being defined. This is not a problem in the sense of something wrong that needs to be corrected. Instead, a program may be written strictly for entertainment. However, when designing this program, it can be thought of as an exercise. It may be helpful for you to think of program design and development as a math or science problem.

Problem definition is a process, not just a simple, single step. Stating what you want the program to do in general terms is only the beginning. Frequently you will need to add statements to better define your problem. Then you will need to read through the definition, looking for loopholes again and again. This iterative process will allow you to reduce the ambiguity or abstraction of your problem definition.

In the sections that follow, you will see how the problem definition for a small business payroll system might evolve. The definition will appear indented, as follows:

> Generate payroll for a small business.

Every time some clarifying statements are added to the definition, the entire definition will be shown with the words italicized.

Reducing Ambiguity

As you can see by the payroll problem definition above, it is not clear what is meant by the definition. For example, what is meant by *generate*? And how many employees may be involved in this *small business*? Right away, it is obvious that the definition is too vague and needs to be clarified, even before the first attempt is made at designing the system.

A good problem definition has three characteristics. These characteristics will ensure that there is little doubt in anyone's mind about what needs to be done. They are as follows:

1. The problem statement excludes the greatest number of alternative outcomes.
2. The problem statement uses concrete, unambiguous words.
3. The problem statement contains as many sentences as necessary to describe all intended outcomes.

The first characteristic should state the goal of the problem definition, or program, but do so in words that are clear to the reader. In this way, regardless of who actually is doing the programming, the goal will be clear. Even if the programmer writing the definition also plans to do the coding, a clearly stated, unambiguous problem definition will make program design as simple as possible.

One of the best ways to reduce ambiguity is to use words that have specific, concrete meanings. These words are easily understood by all and lend themselves to fewer interpretations. If you consider the words you use every day, you will find that the best results can be attained when you use very specific words. For example, a passenger in a taxi might be sitting at an intersection attempting to give the driver directions to make a turn. If the passenger doesn't state which direction to turn, the driver may head in the wrong direction. Or, if you ask a cook to prepare chicken for your dinner, be prepared to eat that chicken baked, fried, broiled—however the cook chooses. If you have specific desires or needs, they must be clearly stated.

This is also true in problem definitions. Instead of using general terms—generate, allow, facilitate, and process—specify exactly what you anticipate the program to do by using concrete terms such as print, compute, delete, or write. The payroll problem definition takes on much more meaning when more concrete terms are used.

> Generate payroll for small business *having no more than 50 employees. Calculate net pay and print paycheck for each employee.*

The addition of a complete sentence to the original definition helps to clarify what the payroll system should do. This is in keeping with the third characteristic of a good problem definition: Use as many sentences as necessary. As you might guess, this definition is far from complete. However, before going any further, let's begin the process of writing problem definitions.

START WITH A "FUZZY"

Robert Mager, author of *Goal Analysis,** coined the term *fuzzy*, which is applicable to writing your problem definition. Instead of struggling with the perfect definition initially, write something down on paper and then reassess it. This first attempt can be called your problem definition *fuzzy*. It is generally a vague, ambiguous statement of the problem. Only through reevaluation and restatement can some of the ambiguity be removed, resulting in a more clearly stated problem definition.

Your first step, then, is to get out a pencil and a piece of paper, and write down a sentence that will act as the fuzzy for your problem definition. It can be as vague as *generate a small business payroll system*. After reading the fuzzy a few times, ask yourself if someone else would have trouble understanding any of the words you have used. In the payroll problem definition, the original statement was expanded in order to arrive at a more clear, precise statement. Since you may not have enough information about your problem to further clarify it, your next step will be to do some additional thinking.

Focusing on Input, Process, and Output

It is important that you begin to think in terms of what information your program will need (input), what you want the program to do with that information (process), and finally, what you expect out of your program (output). But just thinking in terms of input, process, and output may not be enough for you to adequately define your problem. You can overcome this hurdle by asking a multitude of questions.

One of the first things you can ask yourself is, "What is currently being done?" It may be helpful for you to learn how information flows through an existing system, even if it is not computerized. (If you are not programming an existing system, pretend your program will be producing some information that will be used by the computer.) When learning about an existing system's information flow, it is best to begin by learning about the documents used. Each form

---

*Goal Analysis (Belmont, CA: Fearon Publishers/Lear Siegler, Inc., Education Division).

in the payroll system, for example, contains specific information used either for input, calculation, or output—time cards, W-4 forms, and paychecks, respectively. Figure 2-1 illustrates some questions you might ask in order to learn as much as possible about the payroll system. The answers to the questions are examples of those that might be received.

At this point, you should have enough information to further develop a problem definition. In terms of input, you have identified

FIGURE 2-1. Identifying Documents for Payroll System.

QUESTION	ANSWER
1. What forms are used? What information is on each form?	A. Personnel change—employee name; Social Security number; rate of pay; base pay number of hours; whether new employee; number of state and federal exemptions; employee signature; date.
	B. Federal W-4—employee name; Social Security number; number of federal exemptions.
	C. Time card—employee name; Social Security number; number of hours worked, regular and overtime; number of hours absent (sick leave or vacation, etc.); pay period ending date.
	D. Paychecks—date; employee name; Social Security number; number of state and federal exemptions; number of regular and overtime hours; gross pay; state income tax withheld; federal income tax withheld; FICA contribution; net pay (on stub as well as written on check); president's signature.
2. What information is not used? Why?	Personnel change—base pay # hours not used because all employees work full time, 40-hour week.
	Time sheet—number of state and federal exemptions not used because the information is printed on paycheck stub.

much of the information needed by the program to calculate the payroll. This information is contained on the personnel change document and the time card, and is reflected in the following expanded problem definition.

> Generate payroll for a small business having no more than 50 employees. *Employee information will come from personnel change forms. The number of hours worked by each employee will be input from the time card. The program will* calculate net pay and print *one* paycheck for each employee.

Note: It is not necessary to list all the items of information (or data) contained on the forms mentioned in the problem definition. They have already been documented by compiling the list in Figure 2-1. For this reason, it is important that anyone developing a program *write down* everything learned about a system for future reference.

Is the information collected so far sufficient to calculate the payroll? No. Other data must be collected, including federal and state tax tables, payroll frequency, current contribution rate, and maximum contribution amount for FICA. While investigating additional information requirements, don't forget to document information in the system that is passed during telephone conversations if that information will help to satisfy a particular requirement of the system. In the payroll problem, this won't be necessary, because all relevant data are communicated in writing, and all of the forms used for payroll are also used for generating checks.

The problem definition can now be expanded in the following manner:

> Generate *a biweekly* payroll for a small business having no more than 50 employees. Employee information will come from personnel change forms. The number of hours worked by each employee will be input from the time card. *The amount to be withheld for federal and state income taxes will be found in the appropriate tax tables in the program. FICA contribution will be calculated using the current percentage rate.* The program will calculate net pay and print one paycheck for each employee.

The next step in the problem definition process is to concentrate on what the program should do to the input. Should the program calculate values, provide totals, and sort information into alphabetical or numerical order? What sort of calculations need to be performed? In the payroll problem, two have been identified: How state and federal taxes are withheld, and how the FICA contribution will be handled. In calculating the payroll, it is also necessary to determine how overtime should be handled. Overtime is usually considered an *exception,* and it is a good idea to pay particular attention to exceptions, as Figure 2-2 illustrates.

In this case, by asking a general question about exceptions, additional information on calculating overtime and termination checks was collected. In addition, it became clear that the payroll system does not need to withhold state income tax except for California. Identifying exceptions also allows the programmer to become more familiar with what is considered *normal.* Now the problem definition can be written in a manner that is very specific and clear.

> Generate a biweekly payroll for a small business having no more than 50 employees. Employee information will come from personnel change forms. The number of hours worked by each employee will be input from the time card.
>
> *The gross pay will be calculated by multiplying the number of regular hours by the employee's rate of pay. To this will be added the overtime (greater than 40 hours regular time) pay calculated at 1.5 times the regular rate. If the employee is terminated, add payment at regular rate for vacation hours accrued. Deductions will include only FICA, and federal and state income tax withholding.* The amount to be withheld for federal and state income taxes will be found in the appropriate tax tables in the program. FICA contribution will be calculated using the current percentage rate.
>
> The program will calculate *the employee* net pay *by subtracting the total deductions from the gross pay* and print one paycheck for each employee.

FIGURE 2-2. Identifying Exceptions.

QUESTION	ANSWER
1. What situations are considered out of the ordinary?	A. Overtime
	B. Termination of an employee between pay cycles requiring a termination paycheck.
	C. State income tax calculated for any state other than California.
2. How are those special situations handled?	A. Paid at 1.5 times hourly rate for all work over 40 hours per week.
	B. Paycheck written that includes regular pay for vacation accrued.
	C. Not applicable to this company.

The problem definition is now more concrete, but it is still not complete. There is no description of how vacation hours accrue or what other processing needs to take place. This must also be defined so that the problem definition is no longer vague or ambiguous in any way.

A final facet of the problem definition that currently appears to be well defined is that of the program output. It should, however, be explored in more depth. Figure 2-3 illustrates some of the questions that might be asked to better delineate the program output.

FIGURE 2-3. Identifying Outputs.

QUESTION	ANSWER
1. What is the primary result of processing the information?	1. Employee paychecks with paystubs listing deductions.
2. What control totals are needed to ensure proper processing?	2.A. Total gross pay calculated per employee, broken down by regular and overtime amounts.
	B. Amount of federal and state income tax withheld per employee.
	C. Amount of FICA withheld from each employee's paycheck.
	D. Net pay calculated for each employee.
3. What other totals are needed? (What reports should be generated?)	3.A. Total net pay for pay period.
	B. Total FICA, federal, and state income tax withheld for this pay period.
	C. Total FICA, federal, and state income tax withheld for this quarter.
	D. Total FICA, federal, and state income tax withheld for this fiscal year.
4. What management reports should be generated?	4.A. Total accrued vacation hours per employee.
	B. Total overtime hours worked this pay period.
	C. Total amount of overtime wages paid this pay period.
5. What exception reports should be generated?	5. List of all employees terminated this pay period.

From the extensive list of possible output from this particular payroll system, it might appear as if a programmer is faced with a veritable Pandora's box. The payroll problem might even appear too large to be successfully tackled. In order to keep the program definition and design manageable, output from this program will be limited to paychecks, control totals, and the exception report. (The other reports may be desirable, and this desire has been documented. As the payroll program is designed, the programmer will want to keep in mind that someday, when time permits, such *enhancements* to the program will be made.) At this point, the problem definition reads:

> Generate a biweekly payroll for a small business having no more than 50 employees. Employee information will come from personnel change forms. The number of hours worked by each employee will be input from the time cards. *Vacation hours will accrue at 3.34 hours per pay period.*
>
> The gross pay will be calculated by multiplying the number of regular hours by the employee's rate of pay. To this will be added the overtime (greater than 40 hours regular time) pay calculated at 1.5 times the regular rate. If the employee is terminated, add payment at regular rate for vacation hours accrued. Deductions will include only FICA, and federal and state income tax withholding. The amount to be withheld for federal and state income taxes will be found in the appropriate tax tables in the program. FICA contribution will be calculated using the current percentage rate.
>
> The program will calculate the employee net pay by subtracting the total deductions from the gross pay. *The program* will print one paycheck for each employee. *Each paycheck will have an associated pay stub delineating the gross pay calculation; deductions including FICA, federal, and state income taxes; and the net amount being paid. These pay stub amounts will also be printed on a control report. Finally, the program will print an exception report listing all those employees terminated during this pay period.*

The problem definition now concretely defines what the program is expected to do. The fuzzy statement has been brought into focus by asking many questions and incorporating the answers into the problem definition.

Focusing on Internal Requirements

Retention of information for future use is one aspect of problem definition that may not seem obvious to the inexperienced programmer. Any information that is needed each time a program runs, and that remains relatively unchanged from one run to the next, may best be retained on the computer. For example, the information contained on the personnel change form in most cases will be relevant and accurate from one pay period to the next. However, the number of hours worked per pay period may change unpredictably. Thus, it might be wise to save the personnel change data on auxiliary storage for use each time paychecks are calculated and printed. Then it will not be necessary to key in the data more than once. Vacation hours accrued by each employee can also be saved. The information stored in such a manner is contained in an area known as a *file*. Files and their various organizational schemes will be discussed at length in Chapter 8. For now, it is only necessary to specify that the information will be obtained by the program from a data file. This instruction is reflected in the problem definition, as follows:

> Generate a biweekly payroll for a small business having no more than 50 employees. Employee information *retained in an employee data file* will come from personnel change forms. The number of hours worked by each employee will be input from the time cards. Vacation hours will accrue at 3.34 hours per pay period. *Total vacation hours accrued will be retained in the employee data file also. Access to this file will be by employee Social Security number.*
>
> The gross pay will be calculated by multiplying the number of regular hours by the employee's rate of pay. To this will be added the overtime (greater than 40 hours regular time) pay calculated at 1.5 times the regular rate. If the employee is terminated, add payment at regular rate for vacation hours accrued. Deductions will include only FICA, and federal and state income tax withholding. The amount to be withheld for federal and state income taxes will be found in the appropriate tax tables in the program. FICA contribution will be calculated using the current percentage rate.
>
> The program will calculate the employee net pay by subtracting the total deductions from the gross pay. The program will print a paycheck for each employee. Each paycheck will have an associated pay stub delineating the gross pay calculation; deductions including FICA, federal, and state income taxes; and the net amount being paid. These pay stub amounts will also be printed on a control report. Finally, the program will print an exception report listing all those employees terminated during this pay period.

Questions for Clarity

Now is the time to reread the problem definition to be sure it is concrete. Figure 2-4 provides a list of questions that can be asked to help better define the problem. Answers have been given to show the pos-

FIGURE 2-4. Information Flow Questions and Implications.

QUESTION	IMPLICATION		
	Input	Process	Output
1. What forms are currently used? By whom?	Information needed for processing.		Preprinted for convenience and accuracy. Form should not be used as is.
2. Is the form easily understood (both its purpose and its use)?	May have many data errors.		
3. What other information is provided or required to process data?	Must be collected or retained.	Auxiliary storage if retained.	
4. What information is not used? Why not?	May be collected from another form.		Avoid redundant information.
5. What telephone conversations take place relative to this process? Who converses?	Special-case handling.	Special-case processing or retention.	Special-case handling. Additional copies of output.
6. What happens to the forms or other information after they are used? How long should it be retained?			Auxiliary storage size requirement.
7. How often is information used?	Retain on file if frequent. Otherwise, manual input is okay if amount is low.		Retain on file if needed from one program execution to the next.
8. Is any of the information confidential?	Should only come from authorized sources.		Limited access to information.
9. What situations would be considered "out of the ordinary?" How are these special situations handled?		Special-case processing. Cessation of processing.	Exception report to alert occurrence.
10. How long should information be retained?		Save information after processing.	Storage size and retention medium requirements.

11. What is primary result of the processing of information?		Required output.
12. What control totals are needed to ensure proper processing?	Calculate control totals.	Optional reports generated. Human checks for accuracy of calculations (checks and balances).
13. What other tables are needed? What reports should be generated?	Calculate system totals.	Optional reports generated.
14. What management reports should be generated?	Calculate management report figures.	Optional management reports.
15. What exception reports should be generated?	Special handling of exceptions (if particularly serious, could terminate processing abnormally).	Exception report.
16. How much file space is needed?	May have to manually enter data each run.	May limit degree of accuracy of mathematical computations. May limit amount output to auxiliary storage medium.

sible effect on the input, process, or output of the program. While this list of questions is by no means complete, it should provide a sound idea of the types of questions which should be asked. Keep in mind that the results of a computer program do not have to appear on paper. The results may appear on a display terminal or may be heard from a voice or music synthesizer. Also, check your problem definition to see if it meets the three characteristics of a good problem definition:

1. Does it exclude the greatest number of possible outcomes?
2. Does the problem definition contain concrete words?
3. Does it describe all intended outcomes?

A quick review should point out any weaknesses. If the definition does not meet the above requirements, go back and modify it until all three are satisfied.

THE COMPLETE PROBLEM DEFINITION

Even though the problem definition may concretely describe what the program should do, it is probably only one-third complete. A good problem definition must account for the following items:

1. What is the function the program is to perform?
2. How does one know when the function has been performed completely and successfully?
3. What materials and procedures will work best to accomplish the task?

The first question has been addressed by the problem definition outlined previously. However, in order for a problem definition to be complete, it must also state how the program's accuracy will be checked. To answer the second question, the accuracy of the output can be determined in a variety of ways. For example, if a program is intended to compute a numeric value, the results can be checked by performing a manual calculation and comparing that answer with the results of the program output. Usually this manual calculation or comparison is adequate to evaluate the successful performance of the program. In industry, especially in cases where a program exists on one machine and is being converted to another, or when a program is being rewritten, a *parallel test* can be performed to verify that both programs, old and new, are functioning the same way.

The third question involves the materials required by a program, and it frequently relates to storage. If information is to be retained on an auxiliary storage medium, the amount of storage required (in bytes) must be calculated for each file. This is best explained by looking again at the payroll example.

The amount of storage required will be based on the number of characters that must be retained for each data item specified in Figure 2-1, personnel change form. For each employee, the length of these *data items* will be the same. Thus, the storage requirements for the payroll system data elements can be tallied as shown in Figure 2-5. At this time, with the payroll program limited to a maximum of 50 employees, the problem as it is currently defined can be illustrated to require 2,650 characters of file space. That is:

50 employees $\times$ 53 characters per employee = 2,650 characters

However, the operating system will require additional space for keeping track of the file. It is also wise to make allowances for future expansion (just in case), so the amount of file storage space should be increased by 25 percent, for a total of 3,313 characters, or bytes, of storage space required for the employee file.

FIGURE 2-5. Minimum Number of Characters Required Per Employee.

DATA ITEM	NUMBER OF CHARACTERS
Employee name	30
Social Security number	9
Rate of pay	4
Base pay number of hours	(not used)
Employee status N = New C = Current T = Terminated	1
Federal income tax exemptions	2
State income tax exemptions	2
Vacation hours accrued	5
TOTAL	53

Fortunately, the computer system used in designing this payroll problem has ample diskette storage space available to hold the 3,313 bytes required for the employee data file. However, it if had been determined that sufficient storage space was not available, the problem definition would then have to be revised to reflect manual input of employee information during each pay cycle or use of multiple files to hold all employee data. These files could then be saved on multiple diskettes.

To illustrate the procedures requirement, as stated in the problem definition characteristic No. 3, consider a situation where the paychecks need signatures prior to the successful completion of payroll. It would be important to clearly outline the most effective procedure for obtaining these signatures. Either a signature machine might be used (thus having materials implications), or the payroll checks might be rubber-stamped instead of personally signed by a company official. Procedure requirements that have material implications must be delineated in the problem definition.

What follows is the final problem definition for the payroll program. Notice that is has the three characteristics of a good problem definition and that it is a complete problem definition.

> Generate a biweekly payroll for a small business having no more than 50 employees. Employee information retained in an employee file will come from personnel change forms. The number of hours worked by each employee will be input from the time cards. Vacation hours will accrue at 3.34 hours per pay period. Total vacation hours accrued will be retained in the employee data file also. Access to this file will be by Social Security number.
>
> The gross pay will be calculated by multiplying the number of regular hours by the employee's rate of pay. To this will be added the overtime (greater than 40 hours regular time) pay calculated at 1.5 times the regular rate. If the employee is terminated, add payment at regular rate for vacation hours accrued. Deductions will include only FICA, and federal and state income tax withholding. The amount to be withheld for federal and state income taxes will be found in the appropriate tax tables in the program. FICA contribution will be calculated using the current percentage rate.
>
> The program will calculate the employee net pay by subtracting the total deductions from the gross pay. The program will print a paycheck for each employee. Each paycheck will have an associated pay stub delineating the gross pay calculation, deductions including FICA, federal, and state income taxes; and the net amount being paid. These pay stub amounts will also be printed on a control report. Finally, the program will print an exception report listing all those employees terminated during this pay period.

The functioning program will be considered accurate when the manual payroll calculation produces the same results. Also required for completeness will be the rubber-stamped signature on each paycheck. Finally, the files used to produce the payroll will be retained on floppy diskette. The checks will be printed on a dot-matrix printer on company check stock.

SUMMARY

Good problem definitions don't just happen. Each one evolves over a period of investigative and creative time. Each problem definition should begin with a *fuzzy*. By working with that fuzzy, with constant changes and additions to make it more clear, a good problem definition with the following three characteristics will result:

1. The problem statement will exclude the greatest number of alternative outcomes.
2. The problem statement will use concrete, unambiguous words.
3. The problem statement will contain as many sentences as necessary to describe all intended outcomes.

Programmers frequently find that the shorter the problem definition, the longer it takes to develop the solution to the problem. The problem definition that addresses all possible conditions eliminates room for different interpretations at a later time. Programmers sometimes assume they are defining a program that won't be developed until sometime in the future, and that a brief statement will be enough to jog their memory. This may be true, but it is far better to get into the habit of stating specifically and exhaustively all relevant components of the problem's solution. Use as many statements as needed. This is one time when there is no need to spare words.

The importance of excluding the greatest number of alternative outcomes becomes paramount when the programmer developing the problem definition will not have the opportunity to actually develop the program. In order to eliminate the possibility of different solutions by different people, it is good to ask many questions. While defining the problem, pretend to be totally ignorant of that particular problem. Interpret the written definition in as many ways as possible. An advantage of assuming this inquisitive posture is that a new solution may be discovered, one which may in fact be better than the solution defined originally.

Once the problem statement is concrete, it must be checked for completeness. Does the problem definition provide answers to the following questions?

1. What is the program supposed to do?
2. How does one know when the function has been performed completely and successfully?
3. What materials and procedures will work best to accomplish the task?

At this point, it is time to reevaluate the problem definition in terms of what the program is supposed to do. Take that fuzzy and ask the following questions:

1. What input does the program accept?
2. What information paths must be designed for processing that input?
3. What reports or outputs are to be generated by the program?

Next, be sure that there is some indication of how the program will be checked to assure that it has been performed completely and successfully. And finally, outline the materials and procedures that will be required to run the program and solve the particular problem.

Determining the volume of data and the processing frequency should help to identify the adequacy of the available storage medium. Some simple calculations of these volumes before the program is designed may eliminate the need for having to regroup the data later. While beginning programmers may not be faced with this situation, it is possible for an intermediate programmer to run out of space on his or her diskette. Identifying repetitive data may allow the programmer to condense the data so as not to require as much storage space.

It is also recommended that noticeable trends, such as company growth, be kept in mind. Volumes may be reasonable when the task is begun, but expansion may have an adverse impact on either the program or the data format. This expansion should be planned to reduce the possibility of major changes being required in the future.

The acid test of a problem definition is whether it is so clear and so complete that anyone designing the programming from it will develop basically the same results. In other words, will everyone who reads the problem statement have the same mental picture—one that will produce the same output—that the definer would achieve if he or she were to do it personally? When this is the case, and only then, will the problem definition have been adequately evolved from the original fuzzy.

Once the problem definition has been written, it should not be changed during the development phase. Once a problem definition is changed, the focus is modified and will usually require reworking portions of the program. This reworking often results in delays and a great deal of frustration. It is always more difficult to go back and change a program once it has been designed and developed than it is to ensure that the definition is correct in the first place. Please note, however, that all too frequently the scope or the focus of a problem's solution changes during the development of a program and, especially in industry, users may not realize what it is they want until after they have seen some of the results. For this reason, it is wise to provide some flexibility in your program design. It is important to remember that no computerized solution to a problem or a procedure can possibly be considered successful unless it provides the user or client with the information that he or she needs in a form that is both pleasing and productive, in a reasonable amount of time.

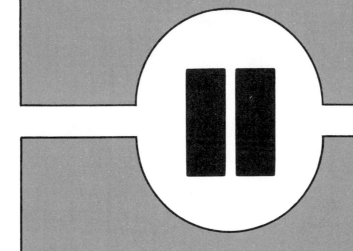

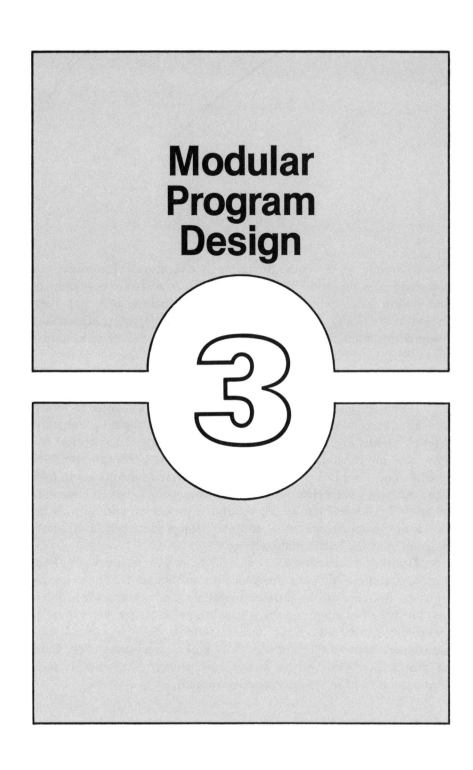

Modular Program Design

3

The technique of designing programs as collections of modules was popularized in the mid-1970s as the answer to software development and maintenance woes. Because software maintenance has been shown to typically involve 50 percent of all software efforts and resources, it stands to reason that you should endeavor to minimize that effort. Interestingly enough, while you reduce the complexity of maintenance by using modular design, you also reduce the ambiguity and complexity of the development task.

If you have followed the steps in the previous chapter carefully, you have succeeded in defining your particular program adequately. At this point, any two people given your problem description and the same input would develop a program that produced the same results. You already know what your inputs and outputs are to look like, and you have a clear idea of what processing needs to take place to reap the desired results. Since inputs, processes, and outputs are the major components of a modular design drawn in a structure diagram, half the battle is already won!

Drawing a structure diagram will help you to break all of the various functions of your program into smaller units. These smaller units or modules will be more manageable, and when a big problem can be viewed in smaller parts, the solution no longer seems quite so awesome. Time and again, design students have expressed with amazement that this lesson somehow makes everything click. Later in this chapter you will be shown how powerful this simple technique can be within a corporate environment.

ELEMENTS OF THE STRUCTURE DIAGRAM

Before you begin, it is important that you understand exactly what a structure diagram is, and how it is developed. Quite simply, a *structure diagram* is a pictorial representation that uses simple boxes and statements to describe in increasing detail the functions of your program. All of the major processing is symbolically described to show the big picture. This big picture illustrates where inputs are entered, which tests they must endure, the nature of the processing performed on the acceptable data, and where outputs are generated. The physical attributes of a structure diagram are shown in Figure 3-1.

Before you get involved any further in data-processing terminology, it would be helpful to develop a structure diagram for a problem familiar to everyone—getting up in the morning and going either to work or to school. Three major steps will be considered here: getting up, getting ready, and actually leaving for work. To be more specific, getting ready is broken up into two smaller steps—Getting Ready Physically and Getting Ready Mentally. Figure 3-2 shows what the structure diagram looks like at this stage of creation.

Control Flow

Notice that the processing flow of the function is from left to right. This general rule pertains to most, but certainly not all, cases. It is up to the *main control* function to decide which *processor* or *subfunc-*

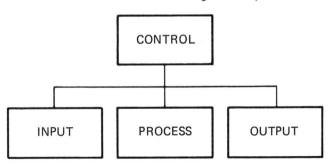

FIGURE 3-1. The Structure Diagram Components.

FIGURE 3-2. Overview Structure of Go to Work.

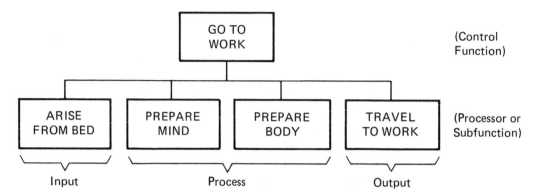

tion box will be performed next. This decision will generally be based on the results of processing up to that point in time. For example, your conscience might tell you that the alarm is ringing and you should shut it off and get out of bed. Figure 3-3 represents control being given to the Arise from Bed subfunction by the Go to Work conscience.

At this point, the other subfunctions have no importance. Only one subfunction is performed at any given time. Unfortunately, the phrase Arise from Bed inadequately describes the activities taking place. For example, before you feel ready to prepare either body or mind, you also need to consider making the bed and turning on the stereo. To show this additional detail, simply expand the processor function description one level, as shown in Figure 3-4.

Here, the Arise from Bed subfunction takes on a control status. It is highly probable that instead of turning off the alarm and getting up, you might delay the inevitable by pressing the snooze button. Once pressed, control returns to the Arise from Bed function because that level of processing has not yet been completed. When the alarm

FIGURE 3-3. Processing Control from Main Function to Subfunction.

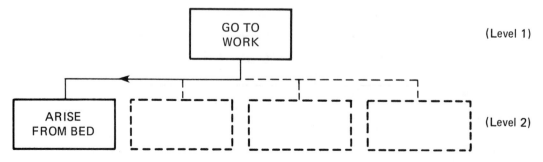

FIGURE 3-4. Expansion of Subfunction Description.

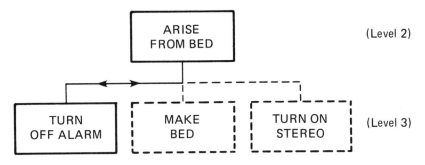

goes off the second time, control returns to the Turn Off Alarm processor, and so on. This cycle from control to processor to control is repeated until you actually turn off the alarm and stumble out of bed.

The next decision, that of making the bed, revolves around two questions. First, did you get out of bed after terminating the buzzer and, second, did you linger so long as to not have enough time to make the bed? It is the responsibility of the Arise from Bed subfunction to decide whether to give control to either of the remaining processors. There is no rule stating that each processor or subfunction must be given control a minimum or maximum number of times. Similarly, it is not mandatory that control proceed from left to right. Indeed, some people have been known to jump out of bed, turn on the stereo, jump back into bed and snooze some more, and finally arise without ever making the bed!

Degrees of Detail

There is nothing sacred about using three boxes to describe a function or subfunction. The key is to use as many boxes to describe control functions or subfunctions as are necessary for your understanding. The levels of detail always progress from the top of the structure diagram (most general) to the bottom (most specific). Often, as you work through a problem, you might want to add, remove, or change one of the boxes. Go right ahead. Figure 3-5 illustrates how the definition has necessitated increasing levels of detail along the individual levels to more accurately identify what takes place when you get ready to go to work. Remember that unless a decision must be made by the control function or subfunction, there is no reason to add another level of detail. In other words, if you

FIGURE 3-5. Detailed Structure Diagram of Go to Work.

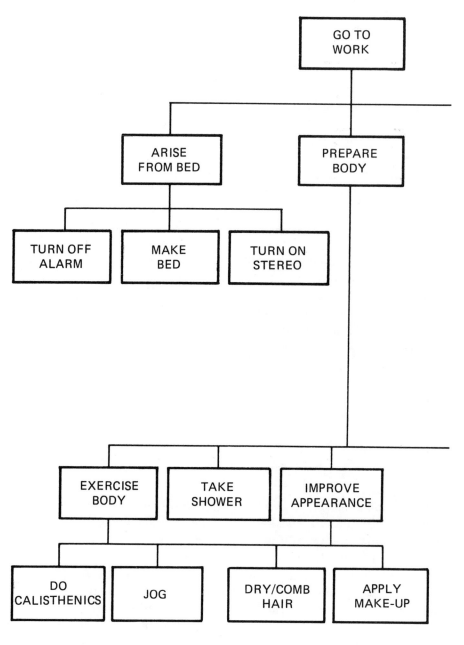

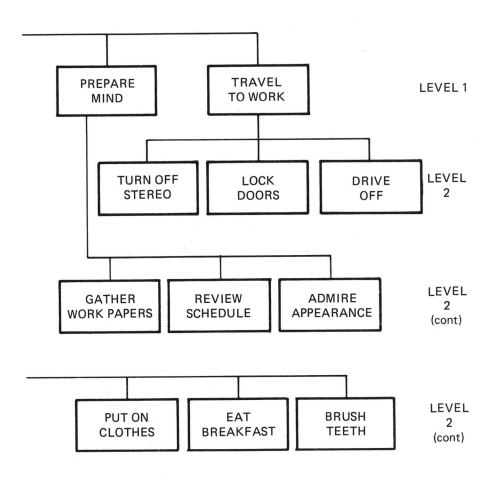

51

have only one box below the control box, eliminate the subordinate box. This can be done by rewording the description of the control box to include that which was described below it.

It may seem that the terms *function* and *subfunction* are totally interchangeable. To some extent this is true. However, the topmost box is always the main control function, and every box below that level, with subordinate processors, is considered a control subfunction. Boxes that have no control responsibilities are called processor boxes, and they are positioned on the lowest level of the subfunction description. Figure 3-6 provides a review of the structure diagram terms introduced up to this point.

From the example, you can see that development of a structure diagram starts at the top. Usually you do not know how many boxes will be needed to adequately define the function until you have made many revisions. Hence, the development of a structure diagram is an iterative process. That is, you must continually reevaluate the level of detail and the placement of boxes and make changes as they become necessary. It is not unusual to make minor modifications to structure diagrams after the actual program-writing has begun. This

FIGURE 3-6. Structure Diagram Terminology.

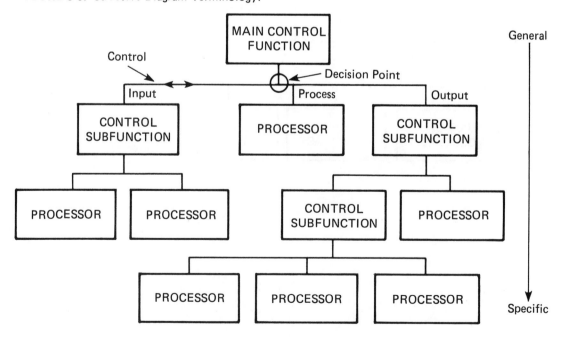

is not only a good design practice, as it ensures accurate structure diagrams, but also a good indication that the final program will be carefully thought through.

It is important to remember that the structure diagram provides a description of the function to be performed. It shows only that certain things are to be done, but not necessarily how they will be done. Once the function or subfunction is described sufficiently to understand its purpose, you should resist the urge to include unnecessary detail. Each box on the structure diagram should equal no more than 50 lines of programming statements. Boxes that equate to single lines of program logic should be eliminated. Ideally, an entire program can be described with a structure diagram contained on one page. When you first begin using structure diagrams, you will probably feel more comfortable with more detail. Feel free to violate the rules, for once you have practiced developing these diagrams, you will find you need to be less specific in describing adequately the function in question.

Descriptive Words

Now that you understand the components of the structure diagram, the general flow of control (input-process-output, left-to-right), and the levels of detail (general-to-specific, top-to-bottom), look closely at what goes in each box. In the Go to Work example, few words were needed to describe each subfunction or processor step. The minimum number of words required is two: one action verb and one object noun. Actually, two is the ideal number. Note that both a verb and a noun are required. Without the verb, the program will have nothing to do. Likewise, without a noun, the program will have nothing upon which to act. Occasionally, it may be necessary to include some adjectives to more positively identify the object noun, and this is perfectly acceptable, provided you keep the statements simple.*

One way to reduce the required verbiage is to describe a function or processor in concrete terms. As you have seen in the chapter on problem definition, concrete terms help reduce ambiguity and

---

*A common data-processing acronym is KISS, which stands for Keep It Simple, Stupid. Stupid is no reflection on the worth or intelligence of the individual, but rather the foolish way one feels when he or she discovers how useless the additional detail rendered itself later in the design or development process. Most often KISS is mumbled privately when a programmer finds him- or herself buried in details.

misinterpretation. Specifically, verbs should describe the processing to take place on the given object. Different verbs are applicable to the different program phases (input, process, output), while certain nouns will become the object of these different verbs as the process flow progresses.

Table 3-1 shows the verbs most frequently used in structure diagrams. The verbs are grouped by program section (input, process, output) to help you locate the appropriate word. The definitions should be used as guidelines. If your definition does not agree with that given, understand that your definition may be just as valid. However, instead of retraining yourself or your colleagues, adopt whatever meaning is most suitable for your environment. The most important point is consistency. Whatever term you use to describe an action, be certain that you use that same term with the same

TABLE 3-1. Module Description Verbs.

INPUT VERBS	
ACCEPT	Receive input characters from an operator, usually in an interactive environment. May include editing or validity checks on input data.
GET	Look for and retrieve a record of data.
READ	Retrieve the contents of a record from a file.
PROCESSOR VERBS	
ACCUMULATE	Tally the number of occurrences of an item or record.
ADD	Insert a record into a file either at the end of (sequential) or within (indexed sequential or direct access) the file.
CALCULATE	Determine results by performing any combination of arithmetic operations.
CHANGE	Modify the contents of a field within a record in a file.
COMPARE	Examine the similarities or differences between two fields or records.
COUNT	Tally the number of iterations of a process.
CREATE	Build a record and store it on a file. May be temporary or permanent record.
DELETE	Remove a record from a file or a file from a directory.

TABLE 3-1. (Continued)

EDIT	Check data fields for validity and reasonableness of values.
EXAMINE	Inspect the contents of a field or record, usually looking for a particular value.
FORMAT	Prepare output records to be written in a form more easily read by humans.
MATCH	Compare like fields of two different records for equality of values.
SEARCH	Look for the existence of a record in a table or file.
SORT	Arrange records of a file in a desired order, based on the numeric equivalents of the fields considered.
STORE	Save a record in a file or fields within a record.
UPDATE	Modify the contents of an existing record by replacing the fields of the record in the file. Cannot be accomplished on a tape file without writing every record in the file.
VALIDATE	Check fields of a record for existence of certain values. May involve checks against reasonable limits.
VERIFY	Same as "validate".
OUTPUT VERBS	
DISPLAY	Electronically show information on a visual display terminal.
PRINT	Send the information to the output device for hard-copy recording. May also involve preparation of the information, such as appropriate positioning on the print page.
WRITE	Electronically place an output record on a file.
GENERAL VERBS (Should only be used at the control function level)	
ANALYZE	Evaluate the contents of fields of a record.
INPUT	Accept data from an external source.
PREPARE	May involve activities such as read, edit, modify, and format.
PROCESS	Involves literally everything that must be done to the data to create the desired output. (Should be avoided altogether because it is too vague.)
PRODUCE	Usually refers to activities involved with output. Thus, concrete output verbs are preferred.

meaning throughout the program design and development cycle. When beginning, it is often helpful to keep a glossary of terms. This provides a quick reference to definitions of words you may not yet be confident using. Appendix B is provided for this purpose.

PAYROLL EXAMPLE

You are now equipped with all the tools necessary to identify program modules and to create a structure diagram for a limited function. Before reading any further, try drawing a structure diagram for the payroll problem defined in the previous chapter. Instead of simply displaying a reasonable solution to this problem, try to work through the development step-by-step. Remember that your answers may differ from someone else's because everyone can view the solution somewhat differently. However, the basic construct should be quite similar, reflecting a good problem definition.

The first order of business is to draw the main control function box and level it with a verb and a noun, such as Process Payroll. Because the term *process* is ambiguous, further description of this function is necessary, utilizing lower levels of boxes. In doing so, you will construct what is also called a *tree diagram.* (It may help to visualize this structure by thinking of the roots of a tree, constantly branching out as they grow, and usually reaching further downward.) As with all structure diagrams, begin by thinking of the function in three parts: input, process, and output. Actually these terms can be used when labeling the boxes as shown here in three phrases describing the Process Payroll function: Input Time Cards, Calculate Net Pay, and Produce Outputs. Again, these are very general terms, so it is important to describe the subfunction descriptions in more detail.

If you approach this *sequentially,* or one at a time, you can adequately describe the three subfunctions, each as a separate entity. These entities are termed *logical units* and may ultimately develop into what are called *program modules.* Each module represents a functionally related group. For example, the Input Time Cards subfunction module actually consists of accepting the operator's on-line inputs and checking them for reasonable values, creating a skeleton employee payroll record, which will eventually be used to print the paychecks and the payroll report, and displaying any invalid information back to the operator for correction and reentry. The following phrases should adequately define the scope of the Input Time Cards subfunction: Edit Time Cards, Create Employee Payroll Record, and Display Error Messages, respectively. You will see that none of these processes alter the data in the employee master record. You are simply ensuring that the input data resembles valid payroll information for future calculations.

At this point it is important to understand the difference between a *master record* and a *transaction record*. In most programming applications, data that remain relatively constant over time may be held in a file on auxiliary storage and used for a variety of purposes. In this example, the employee master record from the employee master file (in Chapter 2 called the employee data file) would contain such constants as the person's name, Social Security number, pay rate, employee status, federal and state withholding exemptions, and vacation hours accrued. From these data you can calculate the amount of the employee's paycheck, provided you have the exact number of hours the person worked during the latest pay period. The input data needed—the number of regular hours and overtime hours— would be contained in the transaction record, which results from the input of the time-card information.

Information contained in transaction records is volatile from one run of the program to the next and from one input unit (one person) to the next. The values are constantly changing. It is also important to realize that the printing of paychecks and payroll reports is only part of a much larger system that would process changes to any of the data contained in the employee master file, for example a name change, a pay rate change, terminations, or new hires. These changes would be effected by other input transactions.

In order to check the input transaction for reasonable values, you must examine not only the values for reasonable amounts, but also the characters themselves for the correct type of character. For example, it would be difficult to calculate the gross earnings of an employee whose input number of hours was *3F* instead of *37*. If the program expects only numbers, it will check for numeric data. Likewise, if it expects only letters, it will check for alpha data. If either letters or numbers are acceptable, the input must be alphanumeric. Special characters such as $ and / are not considered alphanumeric. The process of making these checks on data is called *editing*.

Once you have processed an input transaction for an employee and found that the input data appears to be correct (by editing the input), that time-card input should be matched with the appropriate employee on the master file. Because you want to print paychecks, a payroll report, and an exception report for employees who had time-card input transactions, you can build a file containing those records. You should take from the employee master file only the information that is necessary. (In the payroll example all information is required.) This information is used in conjunction with the input transaction (number of hours) to produce the required outputs. It is from these records (master file and transaction) that the paychecks will actually be printed. This step is represented in the structure diagram by the process Create Employee Payroll Record.

Finally, if at any point during your handling of the input transaction you find a discrepancy—the employee is no longer employed or an excessive number of hours was charged—then you should re-display the transaction record to the operator for correction with an appropriate error message. You could remove the transaction by saving it in another file to print another type of exception report later, but because this is an interactive payroll system, and because this program is to report terminated employees only, you should seek corrections immediately from the operator. The operator, or user, is ultimately responsible for the information used in calculating the paychecks. This process is represented by the Display Error Messages box on the structure diagram. Figure 3-7 shows the structure diagram development to this point.

As you can see by the diagram, it is not important to define the entire payroll process at one time. Rather, work through a logical unit until you are confident that you understand the processing necessary to accomplish that subfunction. Notice that there are no

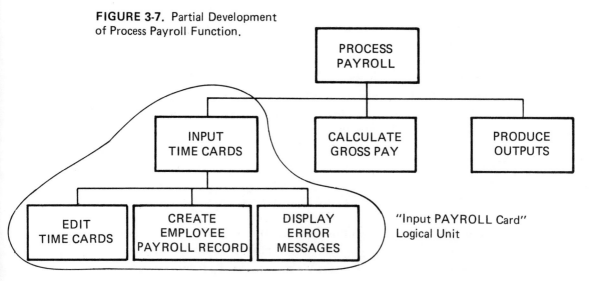

FIGURE 3-7. Partial Development of Process Payroll Function.

restrictions on the number of input transactions to be processed. Instead, assume that processing of inputs will continue until there are no more. The method of determining if there are additional inputs necessary is not important at this stage of the design.

On, then, to the calculation of those paychecks! By the time the main control function passes control to this logical unit of the program, you can be certain that all input transactions have been verified and matched with employee master records, and that all employee pay records have been written to the interim employee paycheck file. The task of calculating net pay (gross pay less deductions) involves many arithmetic operations. Because you are thinking in broad processing terms, each of these steps does not need to be explicitly stated in the structure diagram. Theoretically, it would suffice to describe the calculation of net pay by stating that gross pay is calculated and from that the deductions are subtracted. In your structure diagram you could state: Calculate Gross Pay, and Subtract Deductions (it's that simple!). Perhaps in your version you included calculation of tax withholding, or a more detailed description of the gross pay calculation (for example, time and one-half for extra hours worked, provided the number of regular hours exceeds 40). If this amount of detail helps you to understand the processing that will be performed by this subfunction, feel free to include it, but remember, KISS!

The final logical unit in need of description is the production of outputs. Can you think of anything more to say than the program will Print Paychecks, Print Payroll Report, and Print Exception Report? If you had a second exception report for irregularities in hours worked, understand that you would choose to handle all errors when they were initially detected. This saves on resources and time (no extra file is needed to store the bad transactions before printing, there is one fewer report to format and print, and so on). In a sense, this interactive handling of invalid records under the domain of the input control subfunction constitutes output at the input phase. This illustrates how input, process, and output generally flow from left to right, even within a subfunction logical unit, and how you must learn to be flexible in your application of the rules governing the creation of the structure diagram. Figure 3-8 shows how your structure diagram might look at the culmination of your exercise for the payroll problem. Please note that the order of the output processors is not important because the control subfunction can be programmed to effect printing of either the paychecks or the payroll report first.

FIGURE 3-8. Structure Diagram of Payroll Function.

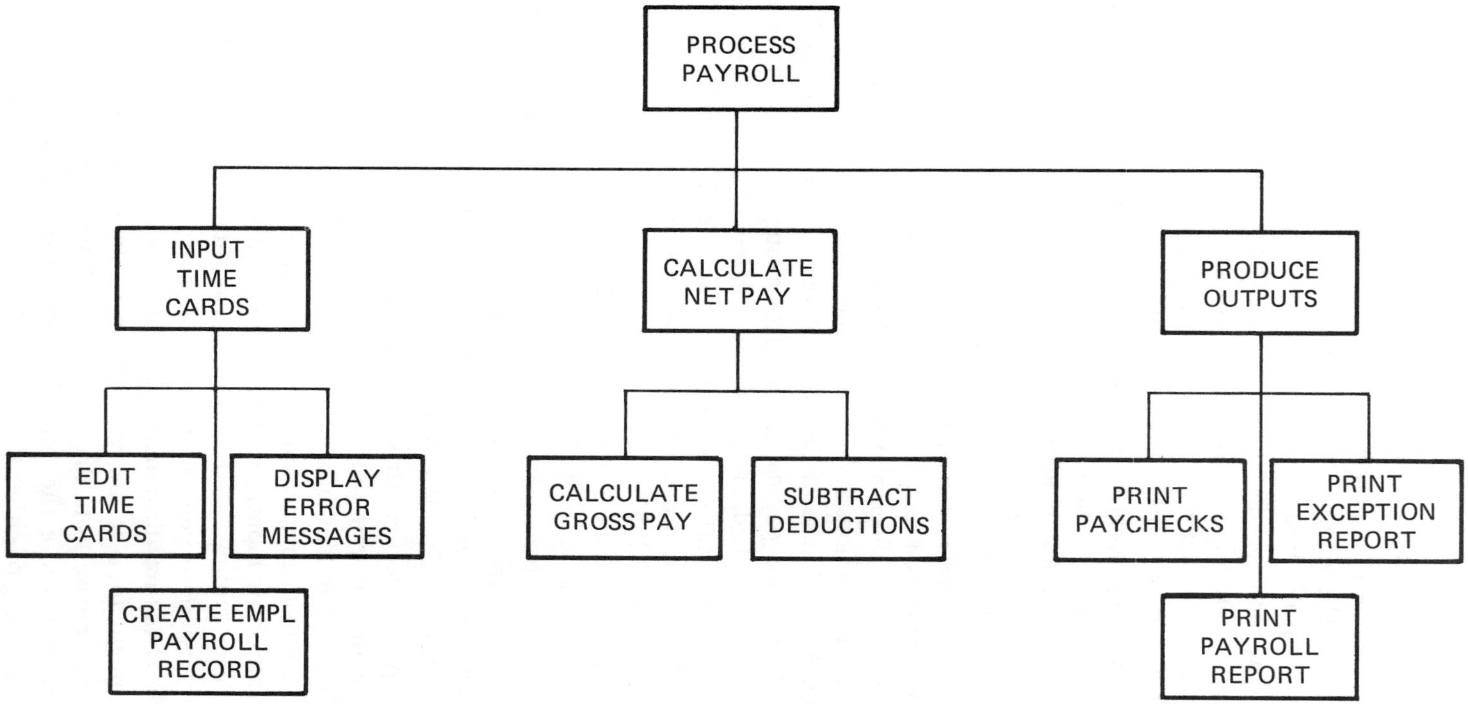

ADVANCED TECHNIQUES

The more complex the problem to be described, the more dependent certain areas of the structure diagram become on other areas. It is possible that a particular processor may have to be performed by a number of control subfunctions, and you may find it necessary to define that process repeatedly throughout your structure diagram. This can be quite laborious. Also, repetition of a process description implies repetition of the programming for that process. In an effort to reduce the amount of duplicated programming, you will want to make that process available to other control subfunctions. Since each structure diagram box or module can be thought of as a separate entity, it is possible to isolate processing that would be repeated and develop it into what is called a *subroutine*. As the program executes, it will actually execute that subroutine from a variety of locations within itself. You can illustrate this phenomenon as shown in Figure 3-9.

Unfortunately, this representation does not identify from which control subfunction processing control originated and to which subfunction control should be returned. You can modify your structure diagram so that every box has only one control entry and exit point. In order to accommodate the elimination of repeated processor descriptions, you can use special boxes to identify where the processor is originally defined and where you are referencing that pre-definition. Figure 3-10 shows the various symbols available, while Figure 3-11 shows their application in place of the previous, incorrect structure diagram.

The common processor symbol is used the first time the processor is noted on the structure diagram. It implies that the same

FIGURE 3-9. Shared Processing Step (Incorrect).

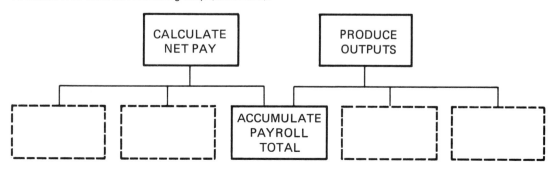

FIGURE 3-10. Special Structure Diagram Symbols.

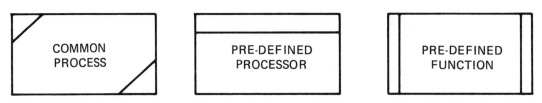

process will be used elsewhere in the same problem structure diagram. This symbol should only be used once for a particular processor, and only for a processor that will be used more than once. The *pre-defined processor* symbol refers to the common processor defined elsewhere in the same structure diagram. The descriptive phrase (or processor name) must match that used in the original definition of the processor. Any number of pre-defined processor symbols can be used, as long as the processor is already defined somewhere in the same structure diagram.

The *pre-defined function* symbol is most frequently seen in structure diagrams describing rather large systems. It indicates that the processor needed is defined in an unrelated structure chart. An example of the pre-defined function is a sort routine provided by the computer or software vendor. It is a function available for use at any time, and does not require any more programming to activate it than a simple routine call. Often, the pre-defined function is sufficiently complicated to have its own design structure and documentation. Although you may not have the design structure at your disposal, associated documentation should tell you how to use the function.

Another consideration of larger structure diagrams is continuation pages. If you find that your structure diagram is unwieldy on one 8½ x 11-inch page, additional pages should be used. Be certain to

FIGURE 3-11. Use of Shared Processing Symbols.

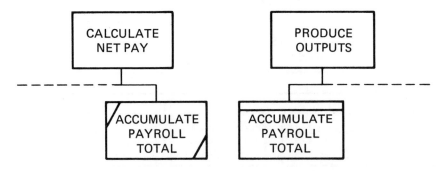

keep all processors or subfunctions for which a control function has responsibility on one page. Split the description between structure diagram levels (horizontally) instead of within a level (vertically). Figures 3-12, 3-13, 3-14, and 3-15 exemplify the use of continuation

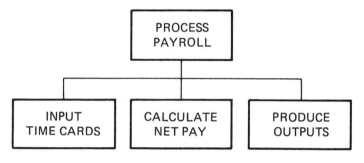

FIGURE 3-12. Main Control Logic of Payroll Problem.

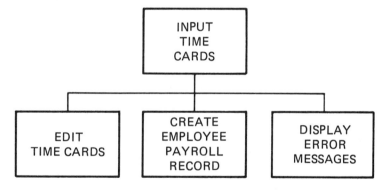

FIGURE 3-13. Continuation (page 1) of Process Payroll

FIGURE 3-14. Continuation (page 2) of Process Payroll.

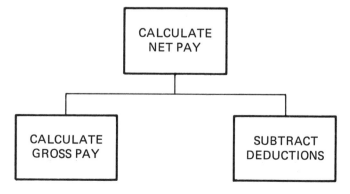

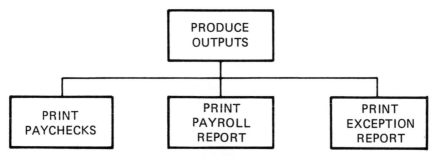

FIGURE 3-15. Continuation (page 3) of Process Payroll.

pages for the payroll structure diagram. Note that when a subfunction description extends to an additional page, that subfunction box is repeated on the subsequent page to provide continuity. For example, Input Time Cards is repeated on continuation page 1.

REVIEW OF STRUCTURE DIAGRAM DEVELOPMENT

It should come as second nature to you by now that the development of a structure diagram begins at the top and broadens in detail as it is developed downward. The top-most box of the structure diagram is the main control function, or simply *main*. It initially receives control from some outside source (for example, the operator starts running the program), and passes processing control to one of the processors or subfunctions immediately below it. The control subfunctions on these lower levels act much the same way as processing is passed to the subfunctions or processors below them. The amount of detail provided in the description of the control subfunctions varies with the complexity of the problem solution being designed. It is subjective and depends somewhat on the experience level of the designer.

To help you evaluate whether you have developed an adequate structure diagram for the definition of your problem, the following questions are provided. Take time to review these questions every time you feel your structure diagram is complete (especially after major revisions). Once you are more familiar with the development of the structure diagram, these questions will become a natural part of your initial modular design.

1. Can someone else read your structure diagram and understand the scope of each subfunction?
2. Is there only one main control box at the top of the structure diagram?

3. Does each control subfunction have at least two boxes below it and no more than nine? (The reason for this maximum will be pointed out in Chapter 4.)
4. Are the boxes below a control subfunction related logically?
5. Is there only one line going into and out of each module?
6. Is a processor or subfunction controlled by only one higher-level box?
7. Is each module described by only one action verb and object noun?
8. For processor boxes only, is the verb concrete?
9. Do the verbs that are repeated in other boxes on the structure diagram have the same meaning?
10. Does the overall processing flow proceed from left to right?
11. Does the processing within a subfunction generally flow from left to right?
12. Are inputs described first (left-most), followed by processing (center), and ending with outputs (right-most)?
13. Does the level of detail become greater the farther down on the structure diagram you read?
14. Are all pre-defined processors identified as common processors the first time they are described in the structure diagram?
15. Are all repeated descriptions of processors and common functions identified by the special structure diagram symbols?
16. Is your structure diagram legible or does it need to be broken down and put on continuation pages?
17. Are control subfunction names carried forward (repeated) on continuation pages?
18. For the processor steps below a subfunction: Is a decision required by the control subfunction to select the next processor to receive control?

Structure Diagrams for Ordinary People

The modular program design technique was originally developed to reduce project development woes from a management point of view, but it also is a transferrable tool that can be applied to many areas outside of actual program design. Consider for a moment that you have been given a brief overview of a task you are responsible for completing. Where do you start? Well, a woman once found herself in this predicament with her new employer. She used a structure diagram to help her identify the main functions she needed to address. Further, once she had an adequate level of detail, she found the lowest level processors and used these to identify milestones for progress reviews. In a similar situation, although in a different application area, another new worker so impressed his manager with a structure diagram approach to a major audit that the manager wanted all subsequent audits to be planned on structure diagrams before they are performed by that group.

A problem in data processing, that of dealing with communication between the program users and the programmers, can be reduced by utilizing structure diagrams. How many times have you heard that programmers are "air heads" off in their own worlds? While some of this behavior stems from other programming activities, if you are a user you can improve communication with these professionals by talking with them essentially on their own level. Since programmers easily tire of designing systems for users who constantly change their requirements, use of the structure diagram will help you more concretely define your needs. Likewise, if you are a programmer, you can help the users understand their needs by using structure diagrams as a conversation supplement. Ideally, all users should learn how to develop structure diagrams so they can establish their needs in data-processing terms before the programmer or analyst is contacted. What programmer can resist the urge to evaluate a structure diagram developed by someone else? They feel compelled to improve the design, which may increase the likelihood that the proposed project will be even more successful. Additionally, any program design developed and evaluated by two different people tends to be more thorough, resulting in fewer bugs and complaints. Finally, if you are a user of programs and find your local programmer/analyst reluctant to tackle a project for you, try doing some of his or her legwork and develop a preliminary structure diagram solution. It need not be a perfect solution, just a catalyst.

SUMMARY

You have seen that the structure diagram design tool depicting the modular design technique helps to break your problem definition into more detail while allowing you to view the entire solution as a combination of related functions. Structure diagrams are essentially tree diagrams, with each branch representing a decision point. Immediately below each decision point are at least two processors, only one of which will be activated at any given time by the control box above. The level of processing detail becomes gradually greater the farther down the structure diagram you go.

The process of developing structure diagrams is iterative; just when you think you have it all defined, another fact or condition is presented, and you must reevaluate the diagram and adjust it as necessary. Some of this modification may involve only the terms used for the module descriptions in the structure diagram boxes: one action verb and one object noun. If a verb is too general, you must either select another word or break that function into smaller units to create a new logical unit. Or, if a control subfunction has only one box describing it, you should eliminate that lower box by rewording the control subfunction.

To make your structure diagrams more legible, you may have to use more than one page. This can be done by following the continuation guidelines of splitting the diagram along the horizontal axis and repeating those subfunction control boxes as the first box on the continuation page. Another tool to aid in legibility is structure diagram symbols that visually identify where common processors or functions are defined and referenced. Some of these pre-defined functions may be provided in other systems for use by any program.

When designing a problem solution, it may be beneficial to consider using a master file to hold all of the related, relatively constant data with which input transactions can be manipulated to produce the desired results. Before your input transactions can be used, they typically must undergo some sort of editing to ensure that the data are generally valid (alpha, numeric, or alphanumeric) and are within tolerable limits. After validating the input transactions, you may merge this information with portions of the associated master file to create an interim record for ease in processing. These steps are all shown in the payroll structure diagrams, but without unnecessary detail.

Finally, you have seen that structure diagrams are useful not only in designing computer programs, but also in defining program requests in a work environment. The exercise of developing a structure diagram forces you to think sequentially, which increases the likelihood that you will consider most circumstances, thereby reducing the incidence of changing the scope of the solution at a later date. Given the most detailed items on the structure diagram (the processor boxes), you can identify milestones or "deliverables," which will help you track the progress made not only on program development, but also on any type of problem solution.

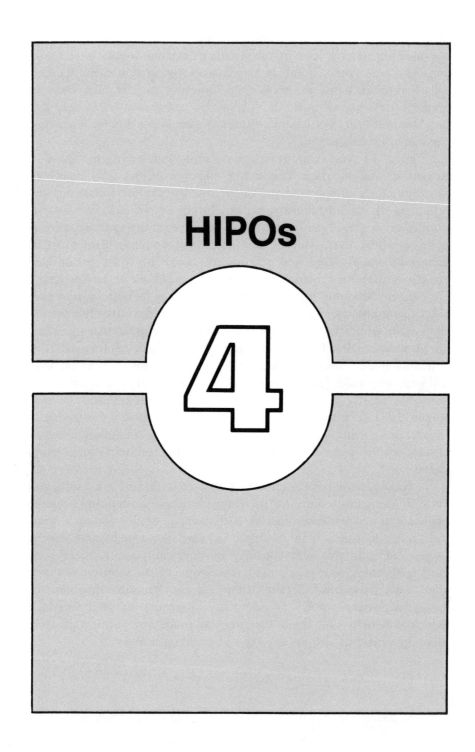

Although much has been written about HIPOs during the past ten years, most of this literature is either too brief or too detailed for the novice. This chapter is intended to present only the most basic rules of HIPOs as a design tool. The rules of HIPO development can be quite rigorous and complex, so for the purpose of this book they have been somewhat relaxed.

THE HIPO PACKAGE

The *Hierarchy Plus Input Output* design package is referred to by the acronym HIPO. Students are frequently caught by surprise when someone refers to this design tool as a hippo. No, it's not an animal. Nor is it anything resembling a hypodermic needle, although the acronym is most commonly pronounced high-poe. While some students may consider HIPOs beastly to develop, with proper guidance, as that outlined with the payroll HIPO development in this chapter, the task should not be difficult.

The HIPO package is actually a collection of three design tools, each having a specific purpose. The first is the *Visual Table of Contents* (*VTOC,* pronounced *vee-tock*). The VTOC provides an orderly, brief description of the structure diagram, and establishes the order of the modules as they will appear in the program. The *Input Process Output* (*IPO,* pronounced *eye-poe*) *Charts* provide a verbal description of each box on the structure diagram in terms of inputs, processes, and outputs relative to each module. *Extended descriptions* are used to outline specifics mentioned in the IPO describing a process box.

The HIPO package provides a verbal description of the structure diagram. Each tool adds to the overall order, and provides progressively more detail. The format of each tool is designed to focus the designer's thinking on the functional requirements of each unit of the program. Because HIPOs are developed in English, they are not intended to describe specific logic (as would be the case if a programming language were used).

Structure Diagram Modification

Once the structure diagram is complete, creation of the VTOC becomes almost elementary. It is wise to take another close look at your structure diagram before you create a VTOC. Figure 4-1 shows a revised structure diagram for the payroll problem. Following is a brief description of these revisions. The process portion of Figure 3-8, Calculate Net Pay, has been expanded to include calculation of accrued vacation pay, updating the employee master record with this information, and updating the temporary paycheck record with the newly calculated gross pay, deduction amounts, and net pay. Because the calculation of the net pay is already clearly understood, it is now only defined with a processor box.

It is important to understand that most computers can print only one form of output at a time. For example, the payroll program is designed to print paychecks, a payroll report, and an exception report. The paychecks are to be printed on company check stock, while the reports should be printed on "blue-bar" paper (regular computer paper). Thus, all paychecks must be printed at the same time, after which the paper on the printer is changed before the payroll report and the exception report are printed.

There are a number of ways to organize processing in order to accomplish this printing order. The least efficient would be for the operator to enter all time-card information before each output. That is, for each time card entered, a paycheck would be printed. Next, each time card would have to be reentered and checked to produce the payroll report, and finally, each time card would be reentered and checked again in order to produce an exception report. This scheme is prone to all sorts of problems. For example, if the operator transposed a single digit, an employee might receive a paycheck for a different amount than that stated in the payroll report.

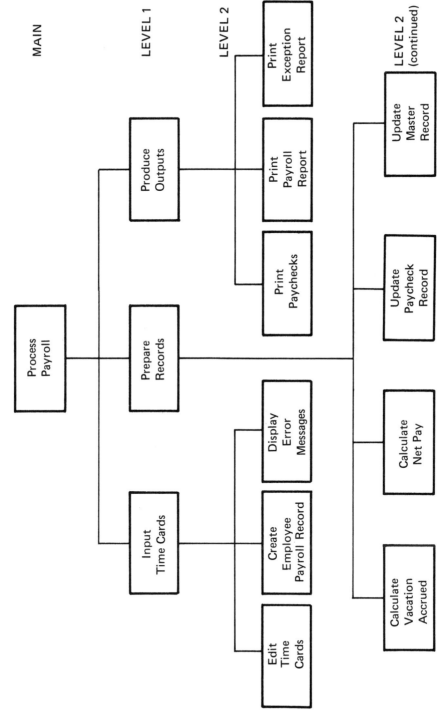

FIGURE 4-1. Payroll Problem Structure Diagram.

The payroll structure diagram in Chapter 3 alleviates the problem of multiple entries for each employee. However, in order to produce the payroll report, the amounts need to be recalculated. It would make more sense if the program performed the calculation and saved the results, eliminating the need for repeating the process. This activity is reflected by the Update Paycheck Record processor. As the program begins to print the paychecks, the payroll report, or the exception report, it only needs to read the payroll record and respective master record for the required data.

VTOC Creation

Once you are confident of your structure diagram organization, you can proceed to create your VTOC. Transforming the structure diagram into the basis for the VTOC is simply a process of assigning numbers in an orderly fashion to each box. While many different numbering schemes can be used, the following method seems to be the easiest to adapt to actual programs.

1. Count the number of subordinate levels in the structure diagram. Do not include the main control box in this count. This count is the number of zeros that should appear in the main control module numerical identifier. In the payroll example, there are two subordinate levels. (Refer to Figure 4-1.)

2. Number the main control module by suffixing a digit with the appropriate number of zeros. The "Process Payroll" box would be numbered "100."

3. Beginning at the first subfunction level, increment the left-most suffixing zero digit by one as you proceed from left to right across the level. In the example, Level One is numbered as shown in Figure 4-2.

4. For each logical unit, proceed to increment the next suffixed zero by one as you move from left to right along a given level. Figure 4-3 illustrates this numbering for the Input Time Cards logical unit.

5. Repeat Step 4 as necessary until all boxes have been assigned numbers. If you run out of suffixing zeros, the number of subordinate levels may not have been properly counted. To remedy the situation, simply start at the top and add a zero to all numbers

FIGURE 4-2. Numbering of Structure Diagram Boxes.

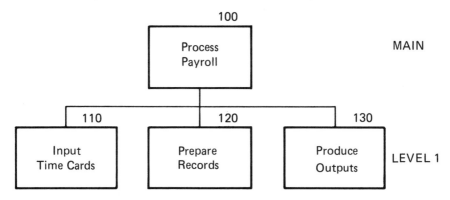

already assigned. Figure 4-4 illustrates the numbering assigned to the entire payroll structure diagram.

The final step in creating a VTOC involves a list of the boxes shown in the structure diagram. There are two ways of ordering this list. One is strictly numeric and reflects span of control through its numeric association and indentation.

FIGURE 4-3. Logical Unit Numbering.

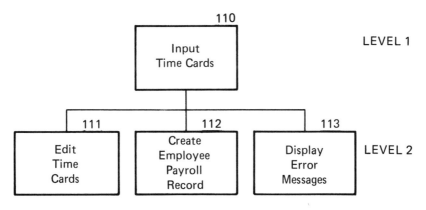

FIGURE 4-4. Payroll Problem Structure Diagram Numbering.

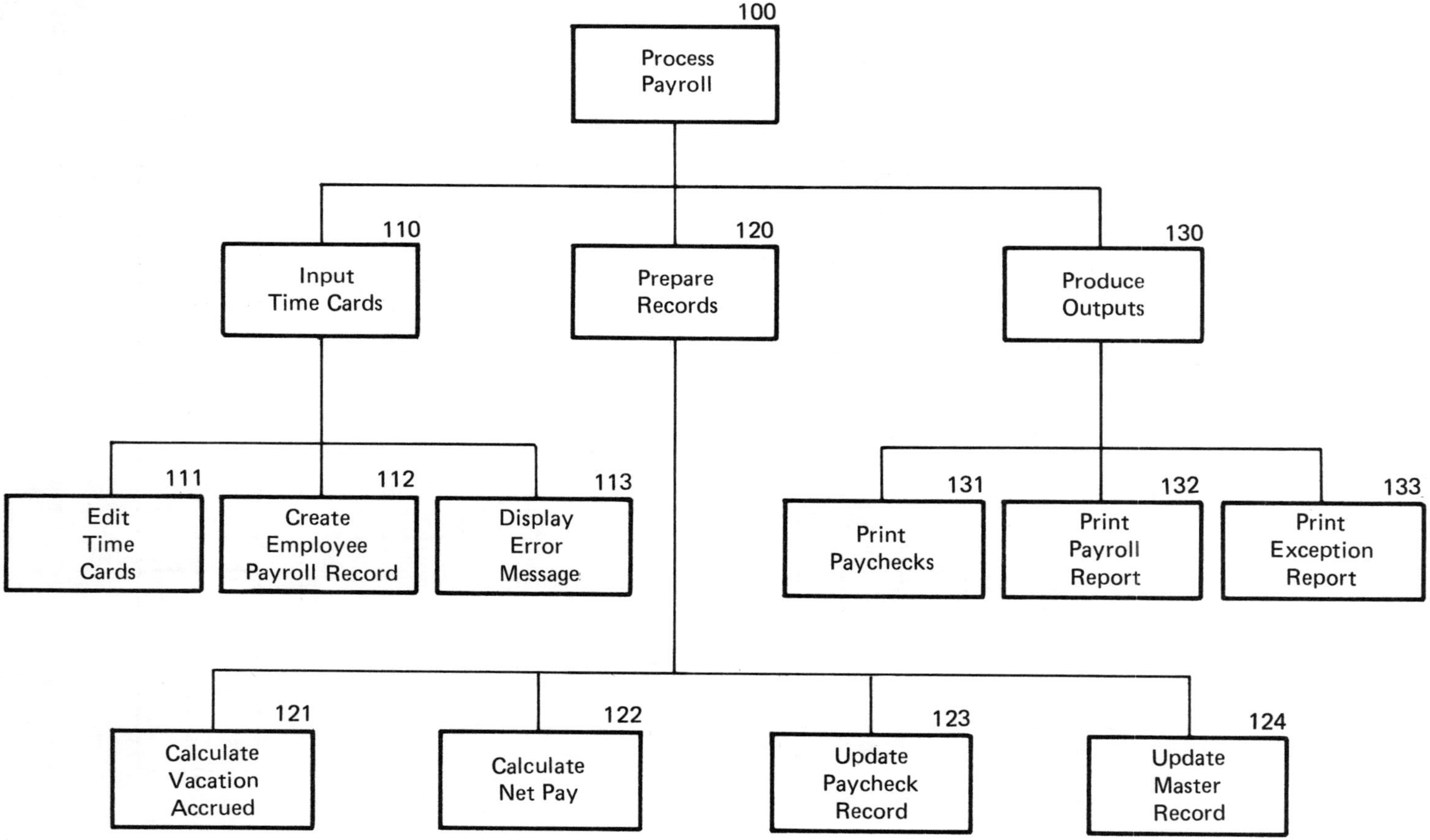

- 100 Process Payroll
  - 110 Input Time Cards
    - 111 Edit Time Cards
    - 112 Create Employee Payroll Record
    - 113 Display Error Message
  - 120 Prepare Records
    - 121 Calculate Vacation Accrued
    - 122 Calculate Net Pay
    - 123 Update Paycheck Record
    - 124 Update Master Record
  - 130 Produce Outputs
    - 131 Print Paychecks
    - 132 Print Payroll Report
    - 133 Print Exception Report

```
120
   121 ⎫
   122 ⎪
   123 ⎬  Controlled by 120
   124 ⎭
    .
    .
    .
```

This numbering scheme allows the programmer to quickly check that all boxes have been included. This is the scheme that will be used in developing the payroll VTOC. However, you may find that an order reflecting the level of detail is more to your liking, as shown below.

```
100            Main
110 ⎫
120 ⎬          Level 1
130 ⎭
      111 ⎫
      112 ⎪
      113 ⎪
      121 ⎪
      122 ⎬   Level 2
      123 ⎪
      124 ⎪
       .  ⎪
       .  ⎪
       .  ⎭
```

In this case, span of control is reflected solely in the numbers listed. The level of detail reflected in each entry becomes more complete the farther down the VTOC you read. Later in the book, when program development and testing strategies are discussed, the advantages of this scheme will become evident.

No matter which numbering scheme is used, as the VTOC is developed a table of contents to the HIPO package is also being built. Because there is to be an IPO for each box on the structure diagram, there is one entry for each box in the VTOC. The VTOC will then provide the order of the associated IPOs in the HIPO package.

Once a numbering scheme has been selected, the elements of the structure diagram should be listed in a table called a VTOC Description Section, along with a brief written description of each element. The subordinate functions or processors should be identified for visual clarity (with the exception of Level One). Figure 4-5 applies this concept to the payroll problem.

As illustrated in Figure 4-5, the first entry is for Box 100, and it contains slightly more information than the imperative statement in the structure diagram. Similarly, there is a brief description of the processing that will take place within the remaining modules. All of the modules are listed until each one included on the structure diagram has been explained. The VTOC is now complete!

At this point, there may be a question about how much detail should be included in the description. Explanations provided at each step of the VTOC supply progressively more detail. However, the HIPO will have much less meaning as a design tool if too much detail is incorporated at this stage.

FIGURE 4-5. VTOC Description Section for the Payroll Problem.

	VTOC DESCRIPTION SECTION
100	Main Control of Payroll Processing.
110	Accept time-card input and create appropriate records for further processing.
	111 Read next employee time card; edit employee number and hours worked for reasonable limits.
	112 Create skeletal employee paycheck record after verification of input data and match with employee master record.
	113 Display error messages for any irregularities detected.
120	Prepare records for output processing.
	121 Calculate employee accrued vacation.
	122 Calculate employee net pay from gross pay less withholdings.
	123 Update employee paycheck record net pay and pay period totals.
	124 Update employee master record vacation accrued value.
130	Produce payroll processing outputs.
	131 Print employee paychecks.
	132 Print employee payroll report.
	133 Print employee payroll exception report.

ABOUT IPO DIAGRAMS

The value of IPOs is that they force the designer to think. In order to complete each IPO (remember, one per module on the structure diagram), it is necessary to list which inputs are required, which processes that module must perform, and which outputs will come from the module. What seemed so obvious on the structure diagram may suddenly seem impossible in an IPO. However, once the structure diagram has been reviewed, and additional detail is added where necessary, everything should fall into place. If the structure diagram is changed, it is necessary to carry those changes forward to the VTOC description and any IPOs that have been created, and vice versa. Just keep working at it. Heaven knows, the payroll IPOs in this book have been redrawn many times!

As with other elements in the HIPO package, IPOs are intended to provide detailed logic for each module. Probably the greatest value of IPOs is the specification of inputs and outputs. Although some of what appears in the payroll IPOs may seem foreign, this is natural. These IPOs reflect the author's design. Another person's IPOs drawn from the same structure diagram might be different. However, certain inputs, processes, and outputs have been selected purposefully in order to illustrate a more experienced approach to program design. These will be explained in detail later in this chapter.

IPOs continue to reflect the control-subordinate module relationships while providing more detail about what those subordinate functions are doing. When creating an IPO for a control function, the input and output requirements for that logical unit must be considered. That is to say, the inputs and outputs for the next level down as well as those for the box being described should be examined. At the control level IPO, only input or output requirements that are *external* to the program should be specified. (Internal I/O will be discussed later.)

Developing IPOs

The first IPO that should follow the visual table of contents is that of the main control function. In the case of the payroll problem, this is called Process Payroll, and is labeled Module 100. Figure 4-6 illustrates the format of the Input Process Output diagram. At the top

FIGURE 4-6

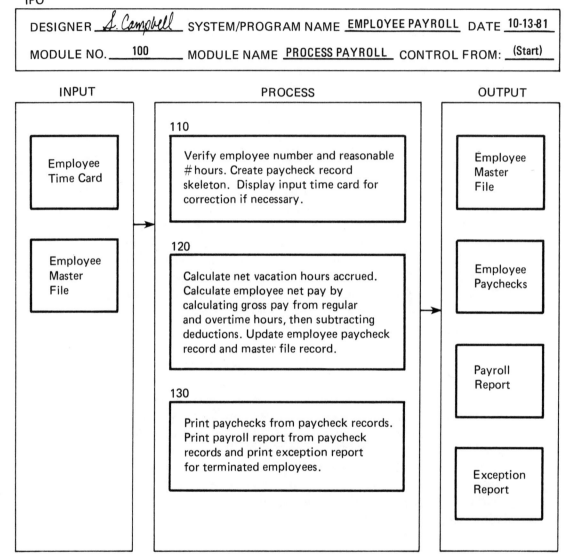

you will see the heading area, which contains the designer's name; the system, or program, name; the date; the module number; the module name; and the number of the module from which this module is controlled. All of the IPOs and Extended Descriptions that follow, dealing with the employee payroll problem, will have the same system or program name and approximately the same date (later dates reflect revisions). Because there is an IPO for each item listed in the VTOC, there will be a unique module name associated with each of these forms.

Take a closer look at the IPO for the main control module. The first thing you will notice is that in the Control From area is the word *Start*. Because this is the main control function, the only time that control is given to this module is when the program is initiated or run. Only in this unique case would anything but a number appear here.

The next step is to read through the input, the process, and the output areas of this particular IPO. You will notice that two items are used for input and four items are used for output. At the control level, it is only necessary to specify the inputs and outputs that are external to the control function. You can easily visualize this if you consider that the program resides inside the computer. Employee time cards are in the operator's hands, and the employee master file is external to the computer on auxiliary storage. Likewise, employee paychecks, the payroll report, and an exception report are all presented for reading by the user and, therefore, are external to the program. A simple box around each of these input and output items is sufficient to uniquely identify and separate them from each other. The order in which these particular items occur makes no difference.

Now take a look at the process section of the IPO. You will notice three boxes containing descriptions of some of the processing that will take place in each of the modules subordinate to the main control module. For example, modules 110, 120, and 130 are all shown as subordinate to the main control on our VTOC structure diagram. Only a brief description of each of these subfunctions needs to be included in this level of the IPO. For now, don't worry too much about what is inside those process boxes. They will be described in more depth later. The two unique things that make this main control module easily identifiable are the module number (a single digit with trailing zeros) and the word *Start* in the area called Control From in the IPO heading.

The next IPO that should appear in this HIPO package is that of the first subfunction operating under the control module. Here, Module 110, Input Time Cards, illustrated in Figure 4-7, shows that control comes from Module 100. This is the module that passes control to Module 110, and is also the module to which control will be returned when the processing is complete. Although it is not specified anywhere on the IPO form that the control will be returned, it

FIGURE 4-7

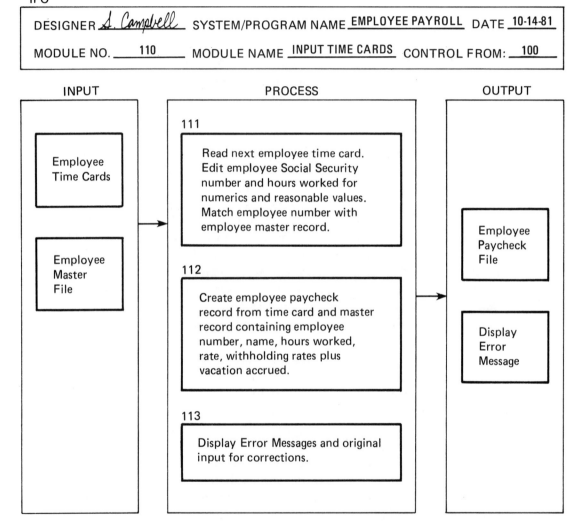

follows the logic that was used in designing the structure diagram from which the VTOC was developed and for which these HIPOs were generated.

For the subfunction Input Time Cards, you see again that only inputs and outputs that are external to this control module are indicated. Note that in the case of the input, it is indicated that information will be taken from the employee master file, while the process section under Module 111 (illustrated in Figure 4-8) references the

FIGURE 4-8

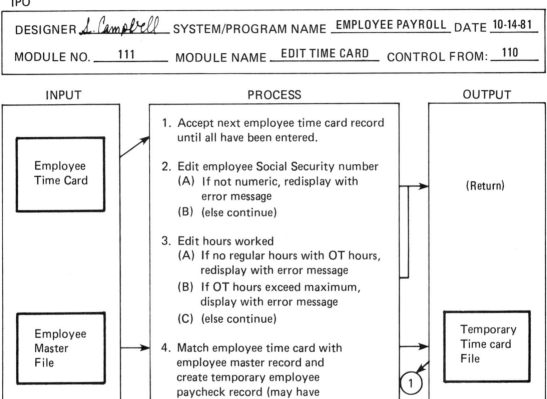

employee master record. Remember that inputs and outputs should be specified in terms of their origin and their destination, respectively, while processes should be more specific. Also notice that in the output section, Display Error Message is indicated. The key word in this box is *display*. This tells you that problem time cards will be redisplayed for the operator to correct before further processing will take place. The details of this logic will be highlighted during the explanation of the IPOs for processors 111, 112, and 113.

IPOs for Processors

The last generic IPOs to appear in your HIPO package are for processor modules. They are somewhat more detailed than those for control subfunctions. Remember that each processor should be defined by its own IPO. Figure 4-8 shows an IPO for processor Module 111, Edit Time Cards. Notice how the control stems from Module 110. When you are developing IPOs for processor modules or for those modules that have control over nothing and are on the lowest level of that particular branch of processing, you need only identify the general steps that will be taken during the processing of the information. In this case you see that employee time cards are accepted from the operator, edited, and eventually matched with the employee master record and written to a temporary employee paycheck file. Those four steps were written in the process area and identified sequentially, beginning with the number 1.

Only processor modules will have these sequential steps specified. The main control or subfunction control modules will have boxes with their subordinated subfunctions and processors delineated in the process section. For the processor-level IPOs, such as those shown in Figure 4-8, notice that there are arrows going to and from the input and output areas. The arrows from the input symbols to process items indicate at what point in the processing those inputs are required. Likewise, those arrows going from the processing to the output areas indicate at what point in the processing the distinct outputs occur.

A special feature of this particular IPO is the output labeled (Return). This illustrates the point at which the module has detected an error in the time card and will set some sort of indicator with the number corresponding to the message that should be displayed to the operator. However, if you refer back to the VTOC you will notice that the actual display does not occur until Module 113. Thus, after Module 111 has set the error message indicator, processing will be returned to the Control Function 110. When Module 110 detects an error requiring display, it will pass processing control to Module 113 for handling. At that point, the operator will have the opportunity to modify the information or to set aside that time card for further investigation. Once the error message has been displayed and the operator re-transmits the information, the control function, Module 110, will automatically pass control to Module 111. This can occur as many times as necessary and should occur until all time cards have either been input or set aside for further investigation.

Some processor modules perform repetitive processing. Module 111 provides an example of how this logic is specified in an IPO. In this case, so long as no errors in need of immediate resolution are detected, the steps in the process portion of the IPO will be performed on each time card entered. When there are no more time cards to be entered, control will be returned to the controlling module, 110. In this example, the repetitive processing is illustrated by identifying with the number "1" where the repetition occurs. (In computer jargon, this repetition of a sequential process is called a *loop*.)

When reading the processing steps for Module 111, you may be curious about the term *flag* used in item 4. Flags will be discussed in more depth in Chapter 6, but for now understand that it is simply a variable. In this case, the flag is used to indicate to other processor modules that this particular employee is terminating. (This is needed for proper handling of vacation time and for inclusion on the exception report.)

In the output portion of Module 111 you'll notice that a temporary time card file has been created. A temporary time card file resides in main memory. Its contents are lost when the program has completed processing (either normally or abnormally). You can think of the temporary file as a scratch pad for the entire employee payroll program. Temporary files are quite useful because they provide interim storage space without using up valuable auxiliary storage. In this case, a temporary file of time cards is created so that the program can remember all of the employee time cards that passed editing checks in processing Steps 2 and 3 of Module 111. Once processing control is given to the next module, the time cards can quickly be read in from this file. A temporary file may be considered an internal file because it is used only by the program being executed. Internal files should only be specified as input or output items to a processor module. Thus, IPOs representing the processor modules can contain input and output files that are both external and internal.

EXTENDED DESCRIPTIONS

Occasionally it may be necessary to further describe the processing steps included in processor module IPOs. For example, process Steps 2 and 3 in the IPO for Module 111 (Figure 4-8) do not indicate how the processor Module 113, Display Error Messages, is to distinguish between the various error messages. This type of additional detail needed at the processor level may be provided on an extended description diagram, which is also part of the HIPO package. An extended description provides you with the means to explain why something is done, what criteria is used for editing, what values are assigned or expected for flags, in what order a file is expected to be sorted, and many other details. Its heading is almost identical to that of the associated IPO, except there is no designer's name and no control module identified in the heading.

The format of an extended description is found in Figure 4-9. This provides processing detail relating to specific items on the IPO for Module 111. Therefore, each of the notes on this description must correlate directly to a processing item number on the associated IPO. Any number of notes can be given for a particular referenced item. However, it is best to put these notes in order of the reference

FIGURE 4-9

EXTENDED DESCRIPTION

SYSTEM/PROGRAM NAME __EMPLOYEE PAYROLL__ DATE __10-14-82__
MODULE NO. __111__ MODULE NAME __EDIT TIME CARDS__

NOTES	REF
Must be numeric, 9 digits (Error number = 2)	2
Regular hours must be numeric and greater than .5 hours (Error number = 3)	3
Overtime hours must be numeric and between .5 and 40 (Error number = 4)	3
Temporary time card record must be reinitialized after saving it on temporary file, in preparation for next time card read.	4
Temporary record created to allow initial editing of all time cards at one time.	4

NOTES	REF
If employee terminating, flag temporary time card report for future exception report processing	4
Employee master file is sorted in ascending numeric order (by employee Social Security number).	4

process items. In the example, you see that the editing criteria for the input time cards has been identified in the first three notes. For each of these editing criterion, the associated error number is specified to indicate which error message should be displayed by Module 113 when the input time card does not pass the respective edit check. For the first two notes on Process Item 4, documentation has been included to explain why the processes are taking place. In the last Process Item 4 reference, that dealing with the employee master file sort, only the order in which those records will occur is noted because this will probably be relevant to a subsequent process module.

You may notice that there is no value for the flag indicating future exception report processing mentioned in Module 111, IPO Step 4. This was omitted to illustrate that, as with the structured diagram process, creating IPOs and extended descriptions is an iterative process. At a later time, it would be necessary to go back through these charts and either correct them or have them reflect the necessary values as determined in subsequent IPOs. When referring back to the VTOC (Figure 4-5), notice that the extended description was not listed as part of the item. It is, instead, an extension of the IPO at the process level. Not all process modules will require an extended description, but they may be used as an aid to documenting what is being designed in the IPO.

MORE IPOs

Let's turn again to the VTOC and notice that the next IPO in the package should be that of Module 112, *Create Pay Record.* Figures 4-10 and 4-11 provide information necessary to document this processor module. Figure 4-10 is the IPO and Figure 4-11 is the associated extended description. As with the other IPOs considered to this point, the IPO for this module has some unique characteristics. First, the temporary time card file is now used as input and output from the process section of the module. This is because the input temporary time card file is sorted in employee order, based on the Social Security number, and written out to the same file space. Sorting is necessary to speed up the process of matching the employee time card record with the employee master file record. Since both will be in the same numeric sequence, the time required to match these will be reduced. Also notice that upon completing the processing of each

FIGURE 4-10

IPO

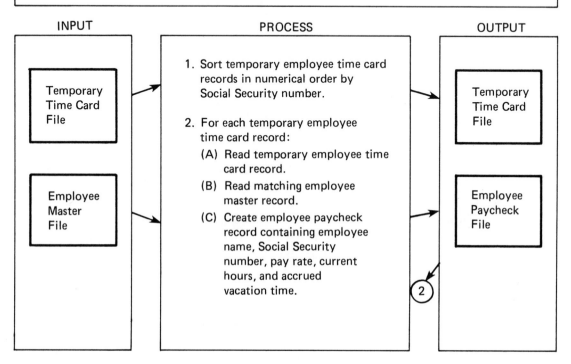

time card record, an employee paycheck record containing some basic information will be created. After this has been done, processing loops back to Process Step 2. There is no need to loop back to Process Step 1 because all the records in the temporary file have already been sorted. Instead, you may go on to the next temporary time card record and proceed through the process steps.

It is noted in the extended description that space must be reserved in the employee paycheck record for information regarding each employee's paycheck. If the extended description is not read, it appears as if the only information required in the paycheck record is the employee name, Social Security number, pay rate, current rate, and accrued vacation time. However, these same records will be used to create the employee paychecks, and if there is no room left for the gross pay, net pay, and withholding amounts, this will not be

FIGURE 4-11

EXTENDED DESCRIPTION

| SYSTEM/PROGRAM NAME __EMPLOYEE PAYROLL__ DATE __10-14-82__ |
| MODULE NO. __112__ MODULE NAME __CREATE PAYCHECK RECORD__ |

NOTES	REF	NOTES	REF
Employee paycheck record should also provide room for all relevant hours (regular, overtime, vacation, etc.), FICA, federal and state withholding, gross pay, net pay, and exception report flag.	2C		

possible. Therefore, the extended description is used to remind the designer that the extra fields need to be included in the record.

The last 110 series of IPOs in this package is shown in Figure 4-12. While Module 113, *Display Error Messages,* appears quite rudimentary, it is a very important IPO. It, too, has an extended description, as shown on Figure 4-13. The IPO shows only one input, one process step, and one output. The extended description, however, indicates which messages will be displayed at the terminal, depending on the value of the error message number. This IPO points out that there is nothing wrong with having a separate IPO or processor module that performs only one function. For example, program designers may isolate an input/output function so that this process

FIGURE 4-12

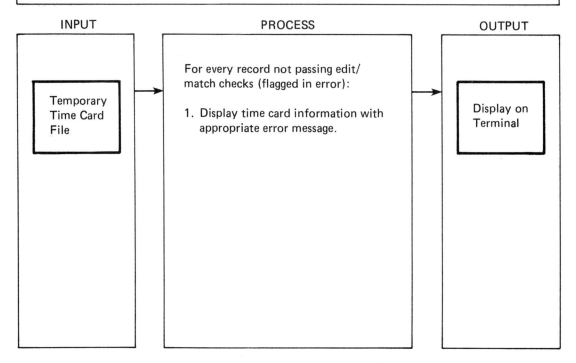

is separate from the body of the program. This helps simplify debugging or modifying of the program if it is required.

You have now learned a great deal about developing processor module IPOs and extended descriptions. In order to conserve space, not every IPO for the payroll problem is going to be included in this book. Instead, only the remaining control subfunctions will follow. Refer to Figures 4-14 and 4-15.

FIGURE 4-13

EXTENDED DESCRIPTION

SYSTEM/PROGRAM NAME __EMPLOYEE PAYROLL__ DATE __10-14-82__
MODULE NO. __113__ MODULE NAME __DISPLAY ERROR MESSAGES__

NOTES	REF
Display messages based upon message number: 1 — Not on Master File 2 — SSN not numeric 3 — No regular hours 4 — Excessive OT hours	1

NOTES	REF

FIGURE 4-14

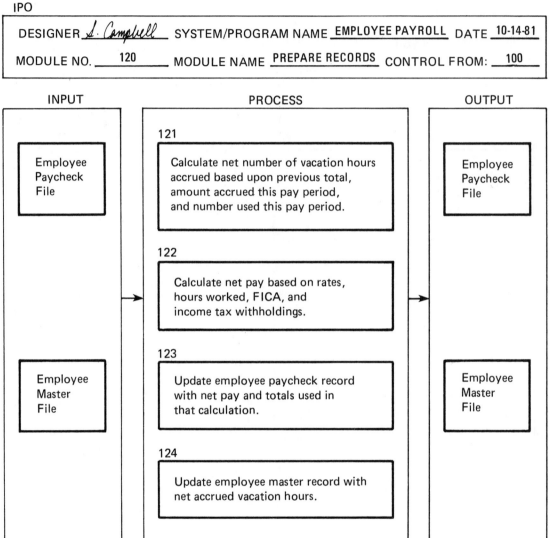

FIGURE 4-15

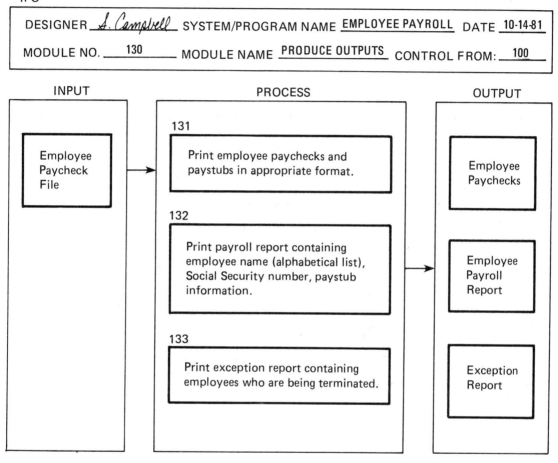

SUMMARY

The HIPO package consists of the following design tools: Visual Table of Contents (VTOC), Input Process Output (IPO) diagrams, and their associated extended descriptions. The purpose of the program being designed can be gleaned from the subcontrol function process descriptions, while the physical organization of the coded program is set forth in the VTOC description section. Each box in the structure diagram corresponds to an IPO diagram in the HIPO package. Location of a particular IPO is simplified by the VTOC, because the order given in the VTOC description section is also the order in which the IPOs appear.

Input Process Output charts are created to help you focus on the process of each module identified in the structure diagrams. The HIPOs require a great deal of time to generate because extensive thought must be given to each chart. Producing the IPOs will help you identify logic errors or where particular functions may be missing or lacking. The extended descriptions provide details of processing, documentation of a particular condition, or information that might be needed by a subsequent processor module. When developing an IPO, remember to address only the module in question. Be consistent with the words you use, and be sure the verbs are as concrete as possible. An outline of the steps involved in creating IPOs and Extended Descriptions for your modules follows.

For all IPOs
1. The IPOs should appear in the HIPO package in the same order as indicated in your VTOC.
2. Complete the heading portions of the form, indicating the program name, the date you are creating the IPO, the module number and name, and from where control has been given.
3. For each control-type module, list external input and output items and highlight each item by drawing a box around it.
4. For control functions, list all of the modules over which this module has control in the process section.
5. Describe briefly each of the subfunction modules identified in the process section inside a box labeled with the respective subfunction module number.
6. Make appropriate adjustments to the VTOC whenever necessary so that it corresponds with the IPOs.
7. Draw directional arrows from the input area to the process area and from the process area to the output area to reflect the flow of data in and out of the module.

For Processor IPOs
1. For processor level IPOs, list all required input and output, both internal and external.
2. If looping is required within a processor module, indicate this with an arrow originating at the output section and pointing to the process number where processing should continue.
3. From each input item identified, draw an arrow to the appropriate process step that will use that input.
4. Draw arrows from process steps that generate the identified output items to those output items.

5. In the process section, list steps that need to be performed for this module. Each step should be stated briefly and, if necessary, documented on an extended description form.
6. Include the extended description whenever additional information needs to be noted for a specific processor module.
7. Indicate in the notes section of the extended description any detailed information necessary to provide an adequate description of the module. Use as many statements as necessary, and be certain to reference the appropriate associated process step number.

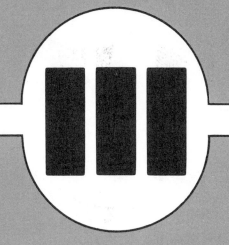

DETAILED DESIGN

Decision Tables

5

Decisions, decisions, decisions! Often we resist making decisions out of fear—fear of making the wrong one. A computer program, however, will not hesitate to make decisions based on the information it has at the time and how its logic is structured. That structure can be the cause of bugs in a program even when the decision statements themselves are correct. Most often, computer programs comprise many decision structures (or collections of decision statements). Often these become very complex, particularly when many conditions must be checked, one after another. And these decisions are frequently not clearly stated in a form that can easily be transferred into program code. Decision tables help the programmer to better structure the decision statements, and to review the program's decision criteria for completeness and logical order.

This chapter will present decision tables as design tools. The construction of basic decision tables will be presented, using an example that is not computer-oriented but which is familiar to everyone. The seven basic construction steps will be demonstrated in two exercises. Then, two additional steps will be applied to illustrate how seemingly unwieldy decision tables can be condensed and made more manageable. Finally, the construction of a decision table for the payroll problem will be explained in order to illustrate the practical use of the tool, and to show how a very large decision table can be condensed into a small table. This condensation takes place only after ensuring that all possible conditions and combinations of decision criteria have been considered.

CONTENT AND CONSTRUCTION

Decision tables require only a piece of paper, a pencil, and a list of desired actions associated with combinations of conditions. Figure 5-1 illustrates an empty decision table with its four sections labeled. Developing a decision table requires seven basic construction steps. The best way to understand these steps is to develop a very simple decision table. Throughout the explanation of decision table development, one or more of the construction steps will be listed, followed by an explanation of how each step contributes to the evolution of the decision table.

UNIQUE CONDITIONS	CONDITION COMBINATIONS
UNIQUE ACTIONS	DECISION

FIGURE 5-1. Decision Table Skeleton.

For the first decision table, assume that you have been sent to the grocery store to purchase either bread or donuts for breakfast. You have been asked to buy either one, depending upon what the grocer has in stock. If both are available, you are to buy donuts. In order to develop your decision table, you must apply the following steps:

Step 1: Draw the decision table skeleton.
Step 2: List all conditions on the unique condition area.
Step 3: List all actions on the unique action area.

The sentences of the example contain both conditions and action information, and because of their wording, make it easy to identify the conditions ("if" phrases) and actions ("then" clauses). The example can be reworded:

A. If both donuts and bread are in stock, then buy donuts.
B. If both are not in stock, then buy whichever is available.

With these sentences clearly listed, the unique conditions and actions can be identified, as shown in Figure 5-2. It is only necessary to list the two distinct conditions, bread in stock and donuts in stock. Although the decision statements (A and B) specified combinations of these conditions, these combinations need not be listed. Instead, all possible combinations of the unique conditions will be examined in the next few steps of the decision table development. The next construction step to be performed is as follows:

> Step 4: Calculate the total number of discrete condition combinations. Do this by counting the number of unique conditions and use that as the exponent (n) of 2. Or,

number of condition combination columns = 2^n,
where n = number conditions

This step results in the total number of discrete condition combinations to be considered. Decision tables are designed to be completely thorough, with entries that are mutually exclusive, and collectively exhaustive. That is to say, each set of condition combinations must be unique, and all possible unique combinations must be examined. Because decision table entries are collectively exhaustive, it will be impossible to forget a set of conditions that could later result in a logic omission (and hence a bug) in the program. Here is the calculation (Step 4) for the bread/donut example.

Because there are two unique conditions listed in the example decision table, the exponent of 2 will be 2. This can be written as 2^2 and simply indicates how many times the base (b) should be multiplied by itself (n), or b^n. Hence, the maximum number of unique condition combinations is 2 × 2, or 4. This number tells how many columns you must have (or how many condition combinations must

FIGURE 5-2. Decision Conditions and Possible Action Entries.

| Bread in stock | |
Donuts in stock	
Buy bread	
Buy donuts	

be considered) in the decision table in order for it to be exhaustive. Next, these columns need to be entered into the decision table.

> Step 5: Establish all possible combinations of conditions by entering a Y (yes) or N (no) in columns for each unique set of conditions. This will be complete when there are 2^n unique condition combination columns.

One of the best ways to approach this step is to keep the answer to the first condition (either Y or N) constant while varying the answers to the other conditions. There will always be as many Y answers as there are N answers for every unique condition listed. Thus, this construction step can be made easier by developing a system for filling in the condition combinations. There is a recognizable pattern resulting from the system shown in Figure 5-3. Notice that there are now four columns in the condition combination section. Since this is the maximum number of possible combinations, you can be confident that all have been considered. Next, the decisions themselves must be entered on the chart. However, you should be aware that the words *and* and *or* appearing in the decision statements will affect how the decisions are charted. Wherever the word *and* appears, both conditions must be true *(Y)* in order for the decision associated with that statement to be true. Likewise, if there are three condition phrases (x, y and z) strung together in the same decision statement, an *and* is implied between each phrase (x *and* y *and* z) thus requiring that all phrases must be true at the same time in order for the action clause to be the outcome of the decision.

> Step 6: Read each decision statement and locate the appropriate condition combination entries (columns). In the decision section of that column, mark the row corresponding to the action clause of that decision statement. Repeat this step for all decision statements.

Bread in stock	Y	Y	N	N
Donuts in stock	Y	N	Y	N
Buy bread				
Buy donuts				

FIGURE 5-3. Condition Combination Entries.

When you reread the bread/donut example decision statements, you'll notice that statement A contains an *and*. Figure 5-4 shows how this case is charted in the first column of condition combinations. As you can see, either bread or donuts are to be purchased, depending upon which is available. When neither is available, the only logical decision is to buy nothing, as represented in the last column. As illustrated in Figure 5-4, there may on occasion be more than one combination of conditions to be considered for each decision statement. In this case, decision statement B addresses two condition combinations and the corresponding actions. What is not specifically mentioned in the decision statements is what should be done if neither bread nor donuts are in stock. In this case, common sense dictates the answer!

> Step 7: If there are columns with no action entries, correct decision statements appropriately and reflect this change in the decision table.

After all relevant condition combinations are addressed, it is possible to accommodate all other combinations by assuming the addition of a decision statement such as:

> C. Otherwise, buy nothing.

The word *otherwise* indicates that for every other combination, the action that follows should be taken. This is an example of a *default* condition. Since a default statement has been added to address a unique action, the decision table must be modified to be complete. Figure 5-5 illustrates the complete example. In this example, there are two condition combinations that yield an action of buying donuts. In the preceding explanation of the importance of the word *and*, it was stated that both of those unique conditions must be true for the action clause *for that statement* to be the decision. In this case, however, purchasing donuts was an action clause in two decision statements.

FIGURE 5-4. Making Decisions.

Bread in stock	Y	Y	N	N
Donuts in stock	Y	N	Y	N
Buy bread		x		
Buy donuts	x		x	

FIGURE 5-5. Complete Decision Table.

Bread in stock	Y	Y	N	N
Donuts in stock	Y	N	Y	N
Buy bread		x		
Buy donuts	x		x	
Buy nothing				x

EXERCISE 1: HIRE THAT PERSON!

The following is an exercise that will give you some practice developing decision tables. Assume you have been asked to hire a programmer to develop the payroll program for a small business. You determine that you want someone with computer experience but, before making a decision, you ask for clarification as to the necessary qualifications. These are the decision criteria given to you in response to your request:

- A. If the applicant has no college degree, reject the applicant.
- B. If the applicant has at least a bachelor's degree but has less than one year of microcomputer equipment experience, and has less than one year of programming experience, reject the applicant.
- C. If the applicant has at least a bachelor's degree, less than one year microcomputer experience, but at least one year of programming experience, call the applicant for an interview.
- D. If the applicant has at least a bachelor's degree, at least one year microcomputer equipment experience, but less than one year of programming experience, call the applicant for an interview.
- E. If the applicant has at least a bachelor's degree, at least one year microcomputer equipment experience, and at least one year of programming experience, hire that person!

You look at this list and sigh in frustration because you know how much better a decision table would be—well-organized and thorough. Further, you now know how to develop a decision table on your own. In order to be certain that the verbal decision statements have covered all the bases, you set out to transform this information into a decision table. After following Steps 1-5, how closely does your decision table resemble the one in Figure 5-6? In this example, there are 2^3 ($2 \times 2 \times 2 = 8$) condition combinations, and each combina-

FIGURE 5-6. Decision Table Setup for Exercise 1.

College Degree	Y	Y	Y	Y	N	N	N	N
Microcomputer experience < 1 yr.	Y	N	Y	N	Y	N	Y	N
Programming experience < 1 yr.	Y	Y	N	N	Y	Y	N	N
Reject Applicant								
Call for Interview								
Hire that Person!								

tion is unique. You may have written the condition phrases in more detail in the unique condition section of your decision table. Figure 5-6 illustrates that those entries can be abbreviated and still be relevant. Also, you can see that there is no correlation between the number of decision statements and the number of unique conditions or unique actions.

Next, follow Steps 6 and 7 to complete your decision table. When you fill in a decision for a condition combination column, note which decision statement you were reading. Have all columns been filled in? Are your decision actions the same as in Figure 5-7 for each combination of conditions? If not, go back and reread that decision statement again. This example may seem lengthy, but it is rather

FIGURE 5-7. Completed "Hire That Person" Decision Table.

College degree	Y	Y	Y	Y	N	N	N	N
Microcomputer experience ≥ 1 yr.	Y	N	Y	N	Y	N	Y	N
Programming experience ≥ 1 yr.	Y	Y	N	N	Y	Y	N	N
Reject				x	x	x	x	x
Interview		x	x					
Hire	x							
Decision Statement	E	C	D	B	A	A	A	A

straightforward. The next example will illustrate two additional steps that can be taken to make your decision tables more manageable.

EXERCISE 2: HOW FAR SHOULD YOU JOG?

Up to this point, no relationship has been established between the decision tables and any portion of the HIPO package developed earlier in this book. This example will illustrate how control decision criteria can be specified for a control module in a structure diagram. Refer back to Figure 3-5 and observe that the control module, Exercise Body, must decide whether or not you should jog. Below are the decision statements that control module must interpret.

- A. If it's cloudy and you jogged yesterday, forget it.
- B. If it's sunny, you didn't jog yesterday, and you have 3/4 hour to spare, jog 3 miles.
- C. If it's cloudy, you didn't jog yesterday, and you have 3/4 hour to spare, jog 2 miles.
- D. Otherwise, jog 2 miles if there's 3/4 hour to spare.
- E. If not, forget it.

Again, this is somewhat confusing. You want to make certain that all possible conditions have been considered. After following steps 1-7, see whether your decision table resembles Figure 5-8. Note that decision statement A gave no information as to whether or not your having 3/4 hour to spare has any effect on the decision not to jog. To be more complete, the decision statement should be changed to read:

- A. If it's cloudy outside, and you jogged yesterday, and whether or not you have 3/4 hour to spare, forget it.

Note the impact of the word *or*. Whereas *and* resulted in one condition combination, *or* results in multiple condition combinations. The two combinations can be readily seen if statement A is broken down into two statements as follows:

- A1. If it's cloudy outside, you jogged yesterday, and you have 3/4 hour to spare, forget it.
- A2. If it's cloudy outside, you jogged yesterday, and you don't have 3/4 hour to spare, forget it.

FIGURE 5-8. Jogging Decision Table.

| Cloudy | Y | Y | Y | Y | N | N | N | N |
| Jogged yesterday | Y | Y | N | N | Y | Y | N | N |
3/4 hour to spare	Y	N	Y	N	Y	N	Y	N
Forget it		x	x		x		x		x
Jog 3 miles							x		
Jog 2 miles				x		x			
Decision Statement	A	A	C	E	D	E	B	E

ENHANCING DECISION TABLES

Now that all implied conditions have been eliminated, the decision statements are, as a group, completely thorough. Unfortunately, the decision table looks disorganized and unmanageable. It is difficult to condense the table in its current form. Try applying the next two decision table development steps to see if it becomes more manageable.

> Step 8: Examine the decision entries for a logical order. If possible, rearrange the unique condition and unique action entries to provide more order.
>
> Step 9: If the number of condition combinations seems unwieldy, combine unique conditions that are always referred to together.

When studying Figure 5-8, it appears that regardless of the other conditions, you will not jog if you don't have 3/4 hour to spare. To make the decision table more organized, you can place the spare time check as the first unique condition entry. The results in Figure 5-9 are far more organized. The first noticeable characteristic in this decision table is that there are no Y or N entries required once it is determined that there is no spare time to jog. Those conditions become superfluous and can be combined into one entry. In fact, you can see that the two decision statements, A and E, actually specify these default conditions. (Statement A is needed only to be completely thorough. With statement A, it doesn't matter whether you

FIGURE 5-9. Well-Organized Decision Table.

3/4 hour to spare	Y	Y	Y	Y	N	N	N	N
Cloudy	N	Y	N	Y	(N)	(Y)	(N)	(Y)
Jogged yesterday	N	N	Y	Y	(N)	(N)	(Y)	(Y)
Jog 3 miles	x							
Jog 2 miles		x	x					
Forget it				x	x	x	x	x
Decision Statement	B	C	D	A	E	E	E	A

have the time.) In some programming languages, this catchall condition is referred to as an *else clause*. This default, or else, condition can be depicted on a decision table as shown in Figure 5-10. In this example, the action entries have also been rearranged. The reason is partly for aesthetics (organized charts are easier to read). Changing the order of the unique action entries seldom affects the logical design of a program. However, rearrangement of the unique conditions, which have an order dependency, can adversely affect the program's logic. To illustrate this, as well as the methods used to condense decision tables, the edit checking of employee time cards in the payroll problem will be examined next.

FIGURE 5-10. Use of the Else Condition Combination.

3/4 hour to spare	Y	Y	Y	Y	E
Cloudy	N	Y	N	Y	L S
Jogged yesterday	N	N	Y	Y	E
Jog 3 miles	x				
Jog 2 miles		x	x		
Forget it				x	x

Decision Table Condensation

Following are the decision statements gleaned from the IPO and extended description for Module 111, Edit Time Cards.

Only create a temporary employee time card record if:

A. Employee's regular hours are numeric and greater than 1/2 hour but less than or equal to 40 hours, with no overtime specified.
B. If overtime is specified, those hours are numeric and between .5 and 40, with regular hours numeric and equal to 40.
C. Otherwise, display appropriate error message.

Notice that the decision statements have been stated more thoroughly than in the IPO and extended description. This is because the decision table has made it necessary to reexamine the decision criteria and to make it more comprehensive. At first glance, it would seem that there are a manageable number of conditions listed. However, once the number of condition combinations required to account for every unique combination has been calculated, the number becomes somewhat unmanageable.

1. Regular hours numeric
2. $.5 < \text{regular hours} \leq 40$
3. Overtime specified
4. Overtime numeric
5. $.5 < \text{overtime hours} \leq 40$
6. Regular hours = 40

The total number of unique combinations is 2^6 or 64. Charting that many combinations would be a very tedious and time-consuming task. Also, working with 64 columns would make it very difficult to assure that there were no repeats. How can some of these conditions be combined? First, no matter whether there is overtime specified or not, the regular hours must always be numeric, *and* must pass the condition of greater than .5 hours and less than or equal to 40 hours. (Notice, too, that if overtime is specified, and regular hours equal 40, this test is automatically passed.) Therefore, these two conditions (1 and 2) can be combined and the number of unique conditions can be reduced by a power of 2. Unique combinations now equal 2^5 or 32.

This, however, is still a bit unmanageable. Using the same rationale, if overtime is specified it must be numeric and pass the condition of greater than .5 hours and less than 40 hours. Thus, it is also possible to combine Conditions 4 and 5. When trying to reduce the number of unique conditions, it is helpful to look for implied *ands,* which are general rules or are applicable to the entire decision process. Notice that when the overtime decision was combined, it specified that condition was applicable only if overtime was charged. This is an example of the order dependency mentioned earlier. Whenever such a dependency is indicated in the condition phrases, that dependency should be reflected in the order of the unique condition entries on the decision table.

Another dependency specified in decision statement B deals with checking for regular hours equal to 40 (Condition 6). This check should not take place prior to the test for overtime specified. It's quite possible, for example, that the regular hours for an employee equal 38. As long as overtime is not specified, the program should create a temporary time card record. Thus, the check for exactly 40 regular hours must *follow* the check for overtime charged or else an invalid error message may be displayed. Refer now to the decision table shown in Figure 5-11. Observe that of the 16 possible combinations, only eight are applicable to the decision chart. Of those eight, the first four combinations are the same (the value of overtime hours is totally useless and regular hours could be less than 40). As a result, it is now easy to perfect the decision table to simplify the logic, as shown in Figure 5-12. The result? Only two condition combinations now exist. By following a somewhat laborious process of examining all possible conditions and then condensing the decision table, all conditions have now been addressed, even in the much shorter condensed version.

FIGURE 5-11. Payroll Problem Conditions and Actions.

Regular hours numeric, >.5, ≤40	Y	Y	Y	Y	Y	Y	Y	Y	E
Overtime specified	N	N	N	N	Y	Y	Y	Y	L
Overtime hours numeric, >.5, <40					N	N	Y	Y	S
Regular hours = 40					N	Y	N	Y	E
Create temporary record	x	x	x	x				x	
Display error message					x	x	x		x

FIGURE 5-12. Condensed Payroll Problem Decision Table.

Regular hours numeric, $> .5, \leq 40$	Y	Y	E
Overtime specified	N	Y	L
Overtime hours numeric, $>.5, < 40$		Y	S
Regular hours = 40		Y	E
Create temporary record	x	x	
Display error message			x

SUMMARY

A decision table is a program design tool that helps the programmer separate decision criteria from actions, and ensures that all possible combinations of conditions have been considered. The tabular format makes it quite easy to organize the decision criteria so that condensation techniques can be used to mold the final decision table. This table should contain only the most meaningful condition combinations, which may be followed by a *default*, or *else*, condition combination. A summary of the steps to be taken when developing a decision table is outlined below:

Step 1: Draw the decision table skeleton.

Step 2: List all unique conditions found in the decision statements in the unique condition section.

Step 3: List all unique actions found in the decision statements in the unique action section.

Step 4: Calculate the total number of condition combinations = 2^n, where n = number of unique condition entries.

Step 5: Establish all possible condition combinations by entering Y (yes) or N (no) for each unique set of conditions in columns representing these unique combinations.

Step 6: Read each decision statement and locate the appropriate condition combinations in the decision table. Mark the appropriate action in the decision section of that condition combination column.

Step 7: If there are columns with no action entries, correct the decision statement appropriately and reflect this change in the decision table.

Step 8: Examine the decision entries for a logical order. If possible, rearrange the unique condition and unique action entries to provide more order.

Step 9: If the number of condition combinations seems unwieldy, combine unique conditions that are always referred to together.

After working with decision tables on a regular basis, it will become less necessary for you to begin by identifying all combinations of conditions. It is important, however, to keep in mind that decision tables are designed to be a completely thorough representation of the decision criteria. Therefore, be sure that nothing has been left out. And good luck!

Flowcharting 6

Did you ever stop to think about how many discrete steps are involved in writing your name, getting dressed, taking a shower, or driving a car? Each one of these tasks may seem quite routine, but each requires a set of discrete actions to be performed in a particular order. Such is the case with a computer program. These individual, sequential steps—some including simple processes, some far more complex, and many requiring that decisions be made at particular points—comprise the logic of the program. Unlike human beings, computers must be instructed to perform each and every step. Up to this point, the logic-design tools have been general in nature (structure diagrams and HIPOs). While decision tables are quite detailed, they have not been integrated into the logic-design process. This chapter on flowcharting will explore program design on a detailed logic level, and show how processes and decisions are combined to form a program, in pictures.

A *flowchart* is an illustration with a few words of explanation that describes the sequence of steps required to perform a particular function. Flowcharts can be thought of as maps, or legends, to programs. Different shaped symbols—for example, circles, rectangles, ellipses and diamonds—are assigned special meanings so that the number of descriptive words is minimized (remember: A picture is worth a thousand words!). These shapes are called *flowchart symbols*. Flowcharts are fun to draw, and they allow you to quickly review the logic of your program before you expend effort on coding. It is much easier to identify where a line should be moved on a flowchart than it is to identify where a line of code should be moved. Hence, flowcharts should be prepared *before* the program is coded. Unfortunately, some programs are written without the aid of a flowchart, and when this occurs, the programmer may find him- or herself knee-deep in program logic with no idea where to go next. In times like this, an after-the-fact flowchart can be useful in helping the programmer better understand these troublesome areas. This is particularly true when facing a complex program written by someone else.

This chapter will introduce the most frequently used flowchart symbols, and then show how they are used to provide a pictorial representation of program logic in progressively more detail. Basic flowchart constructs of processes, decisions, and loops will be examined, as well as more advanced techniques of subroutines and continuation pages. Finally, flowcharting will be related to decision tables and IPO diagrams.

SYMBOLOGY

Before diving into the payroll problem, sequential processes and flowcharting will be explained through a task common to all: taking a shower. Please note that this function relates back to the Go to Work structure diagram shown in Figure 3-5. For a moment, think of all the steps required to successfully complete the task at hand—taking a shower. (It is assumed here that a successful shower is indicated by a clean, dry, and unclad individual emerging from the tub or stall.) Generally speaking, these are the steps required:

1. Turn on water
2. Remove clothes
3. Get into shower
4. Wash and rinse hair and body
5. Turn off water
6. Towel dry hair and body
7. Get out of shower

Figure 6-1 shows a flowchart of the sequential process of taking a shower. You should note that these steps need not necessarily occur in the order specified. For instance, some people prefer to turn on the shower water either after removing their clothes or after they have already entered the shower. If either of these options were selected, the flowchart would need to be altered to reflect that particular sequence. This particular process seems fairly straightforward, with each step appearing in simple rectangular symbols.

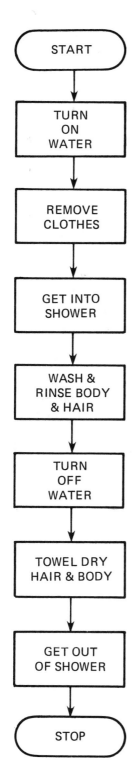

FIGURE 6-1. Flowchart Depicting the Taking of a Shower.

However, what is lacking from this flowchart is a level of detail sufficient to describe the logic involved in a) ensuring that the water temperature is comfortable, b) ensuring that the washing of hair and body is adequate, and c) determining that the hair and body are sufficiently dry. Each of these requires only the addition of some simple decision criteria, as illustrated in Figure 6-2. As you can see, the criteria for successful completion of the shower process is now specified in logic flow. Note how difficult it is to insert verbiage into the individual flowchart symbols. You may find it easier to place the descriptive text outside and to the right of the flowchart symbols. In order for some of the flowcharts in this book to be more easily read, they will be drawn with the symbols placed to the left and the supporting text will be placed to the right of the symbol.

As you may have surmised, the rectangular (▭) symbol is used to illustrate a process step. A diamond (◇) represents a binary (yes or no) decision point. Ellipses (⬭) denote beginning and ending flow, or terminal, points, and arrows are used to show in which direction processing should continue. These are the most commonly used flowchart symbols. A complete array of ANSI standard flowchart symbols is presented in Appendix C. Many of these symbols will be described later in this chapter.

In the figures presented so far, you will note that all connecting lines are accompanied by directional arrows. In this book, the processing flow is assumed to proceed from the top to the bottom of the page, and from the left to the right. If the flow must go bottom-up or right-left, directional arrows must be shown. Otherwise, they may be implied.

The decision condition (yes or no) for a decision point must be specified for each connector, leaving the decision symbol as shown in Figure 6-3. It is not important whether all *no* conditions result in downward movement along a flowchart, or that the horizontal departure results in a previous or past reentry connection (see Figure 6-4). What is important is that the flowchart be as easy to read as possible. By striving for consistency in flowcharting, you will produce more legible, logical results.

Progressive Degrees of Detail

One of the major advantages of flowcharts is the pictorial representation of program logic in greater degrees of detail. The American National Standards Institute (ANSI), together with the International Standards Organization (ISO), have recommended standard flow-

FIGURE 6-2. Additional Shower Detail.

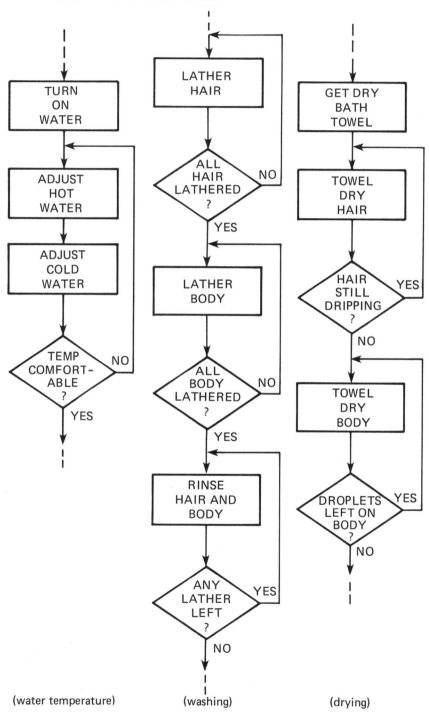

(water temperature)   (washing)   (drying)

117

FIGURE 6-3. Decision Point Characteristics.

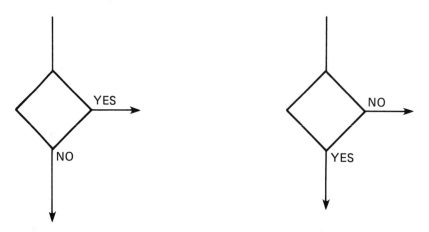

chart symbols and techniques. The symbols can be grouped into two general categories of symbols: system and program. While this distinction may be important in a large system-development environment, the most frequently used system and program flowchart symbols can be combined to readily document the interactive nature of many microcomputer programs. No distinction between system and program flowchart symbols must be made. However, it is important to understand the difference in detail depicted by system and program level flowcharts. Figure 6-5 shows the expansion of the Process Payroll function in the payroll system flowchart. Each of the process boxes in the system flowchart can be further expanded to

FIGURE 6-4. Decision Point Reentry Directions.

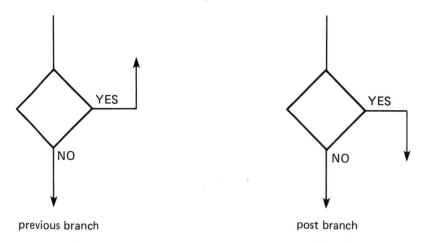

previous branch	post branch

FIGURE 6-5. System vs. Program Flowcharts.

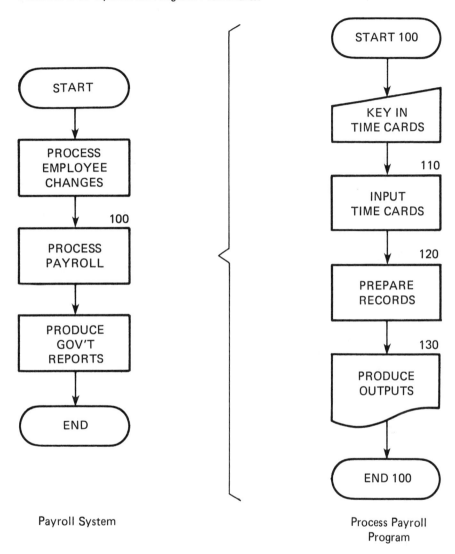

Payroll System

Process Payroll Program

provide more detail on how that function will actually occur. For example, if more detail is needed on the 120 Prepare Records sub-function, a flowchart could be drawn to show that.

When you begin to draw a flowchart of a system or program, it isn't necessary that you fully understand how a function or process is to be performed. It is more important that you conceptually know it can be done. Then, without going into detail, you can show where it is to be performed in the overall scheme or function by drawing a process box with the function name. In this case, the process is known as a *black box*.

Flowchart Constructs

Thus far you have learned how flowcharts are used to indicate both how and where a function is to be performed within the sequential flow of the system or program. In order to show how frequently or when a function or program step should be performed, certain combinations of flowchart symbols and conditions are constructed. According to Bohm and Jacopini, only three basic constructs need be employed. These are the simple process, the binary decision, and the loop. Figure 6-6 illustrates these constructs.

Because flowcharts reflect the sequential nature of programs, each of these constructs will be performed in your program whenever processing or *program execution* reaches that point represented by that flowchart construct. This is simple to understand for the process construct, as it will always be performed after the construct preceding it in the flowchart and before the construct following it.

Interpreting the *binary decision* (also referred to as the if-then-else) construct is slightly more complex. In order to determine when each process (B or C) will be performed (refer to Figure 6-6), you must determine the results of the binary decision point (b) at the top of the construct. The total number of times both B and C are performed will equal the number of times the decision point (b) is executed.

The origin of the term *loop* can be seen in Figure 6-6. Every time the decision at (d) results in the subsequent execution of black box D, a loop in the program has been executed. The number of times this loop is traversed depends on the decision criteria at point (d). On some occasions, the criteria will be based upon a particular number. For example, assume that the payroll program must produce paychecks for exactly 12 employees, and they are the only individuals on the employee master file. The loop for reading the master file records could then be drawn as shown in Figure 6-7. Usually it is best not to lock your program into a set number of iterations of loops. In this example, if the number of employees exceeded 12, not all master-file records for active employees would be read. Figure 6-8 illustrates three different ways of performing loops. The first method illustrated is called the accumulator method. After each record is read, an *accumulator*, or *counter* (NUMEMP), is

FIGURE 6-6. Three Basic Flowchart Constructs.

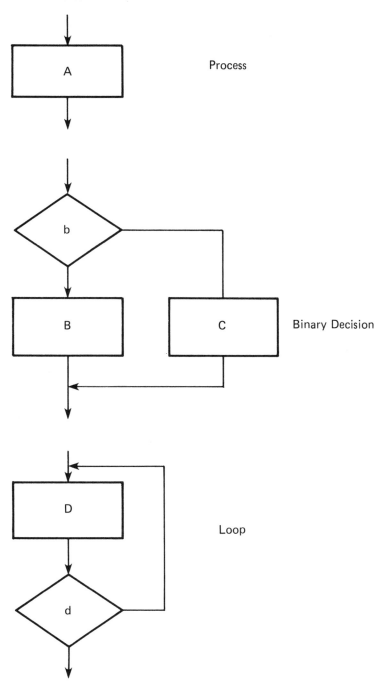

FIGURE 6-7. Loop Constant Number of Times.

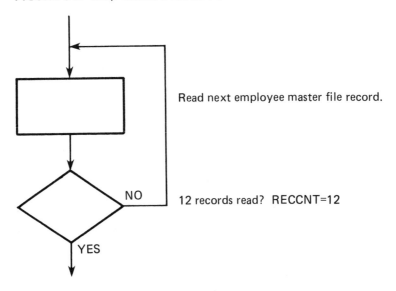

incremented (one is added to its value) and checked for a specific value. When a specific value is coded in the program logic, it is said to be *hard coded*. Hard coding values may be desirable in isolated cases. However, when that same value is checked in a variety of places in the program it is advisable to check the value against a variable. This variable may have its value initialized by some external source (card read, operator-keyed), or it may be initially set or *initialized* to a value at one place in the program. This isolation of value-setting allows for a quicker change should it become necessary—it's faster to change one line of code than it is to change dozens. Also, if the value were hard coded in dozens of places, the chances of locating all statements is greatly reduced. Hence, it is wise to anticipate the fluctuation of values so the program does not need to be modified and recompiled each time the value changes.

You may notice some new symbols in this flowchart, namely the preparation box (⬔), the same-page connector (○) and the other-page connector (⌂). Preparation symbols are used to indicate where, typically, data fields or variables are set to specific values. In the accumulator example, the variable NUMEMP is initialized to zero. The connector symbols are fairly self-explanatory. Connectors should be labeled uniquely and should correspond to the respective page identifier. In this case, it's assumed that the flowcharts are drawn on page A and that the connector A1 is the first connector to appear. Further, the identifier A will be included in the label of the program code at this logical point. Other-page connectors should identify specific connectors, like B4, when appropriate.

FIGURE 6-8. Loop Limitation Methods.

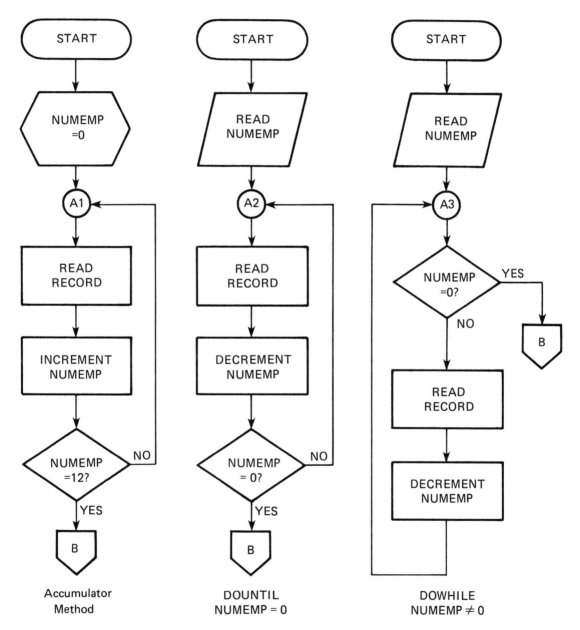

In the DOUNTIL and DOWHILE examples of looping methods shown in Figure 6-8, the number of employees (NUMEMP) to process is read in by the program. This method of loop control provides flexibility so that the program does not have to be changed should the number of employees change. In both cases you'll notice that the *counter* NUMEMP is decremented (one is subtracted from the value) until the appropriate number of employee records has been read (NUMEMP = 0).

The basic difference between DOWHILE and DOUNTIL loops hinges on when the loop test is made. That is to say, a DOWHILE loop tests the decision condition after processing has occurred, while the DOUNTIL tests the condition before the function is performed. You should be careful when using DOUNTIL loops because it is possible that the function or process should not be performed even once (for example, if NUMEMP = 0 initially). The DOWHILE protects your program from this potential bug by performing the condition test first.

Subroutines

Another advantage of flowcharts is that they facilitate the identification of repetitive processes. That is, when the same set of logic is needed in a variety of places in your flowchart, the repetition of this logic set is easy to identify. The process steps in your flowchart will have the same picture each time they appear in the flowchart. When you identify such a process, you can isolate this set of processing into what is called a *subroutine* or *module*. Subroutines can be executed from any point in your program. Each execution begins at the subroutine entry point and ends at the exit point. Processing then normally continues at the instruction immediately following the instruction that triggered the execution of (or that *called*) the subroutine.

Showing a call to a subroutine or module is not unlike a structure diagram predefined process. In flowcharting, you only need to flowchart the steps in the subroutine once. This flowchart should be named and appear on a separate page. Then, in other areas of your program flowchart you can refer to that subroutine as though it were a black box. To highlight the fact that the black box is actually a subroutine, a bar should be drawn across the top portion of the process rectangle. The name of the subroutine should also be indicated, as shown in Figure 6-9 for subroutine DISPERR. Each time this subroutine is called, an error message will be presented on the

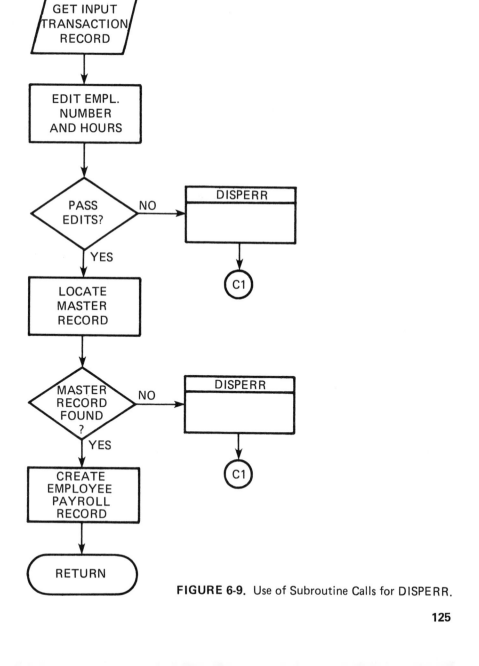

FIGURE 6-9. Use of Subroutine Calls for DISPERR.

display unit describing to the operator what error the program detected. Figure 4-13 shows a list of error messages that will be displayed based on the value of a variable. The flowchart in Figure 6-10 shows one way that the logic can be designed to effect this scheme, using the variable DISPNUM to indicate which error message should be displayed.

This example also uses another flowchart symbol: the display symbol (◯). This subroutine could also accept the input of the data that had been found incorrect, although this logic is not specified here. Notice also how the decisions are strung together—one right after the other—and how each decision is based on the value of the same variable, in this example DISPNUM. This flowchart construct has a special name. It is called *case logic*. In Figure 6-10, the logic only covers the cases when DISPNUM is equal to 1, 2, 3, or 4. What would this subroutine do if the value or case of DISPNUM equalled 0 or 5? It would "fall through" the decision points and simply return, with no notification of the error condition being given to the operator. For this reason, it is best to include one other case, sort of a catchall case. Figure 6-11 shows the addition of *idiot check* logic to alert the operator that the program has a bug.

Flowcharting Decision Tables

To show how decision tables are flowcharted, refer to Figure 5-7 for the Hire that Person decision table. Remember that the purpose of decision tables is to ensure that all possible combinations of conditions are accounted for in the program design. As you can see from Figure 6-12, combinations of decisions can get rather complicated. However, the logic paths through the flowchart can be checked against each unique combination of conditions, as shown in the decision table. Further, the logic can be arranged—that is, the order of the decision conditions can be arranged to optimize the program code. Once you have worked with flowcharts for a while, you will learn to organize the decision criteria to eliminate the greatest number of condition combinations first. Usually, this has the effect of simplifying your flowchart, and has the corresponding effect of simplifying the program coding.

An example of this simplification is shown in Figure 6-13. This flowchart corresponds to the decision table shown in Figure 5-12. All possible combinations of conditions are accounted for in this example. While all the resultant error messages have not been specified, each case results in a different value being assigned to the error

FIGURE 6-10. DISPERR Subroutine Flowchart.

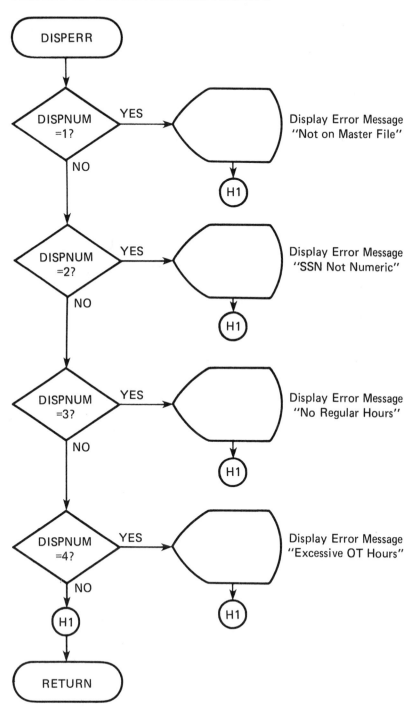

FIGURE 6-11. DISPERR Subroutine with Bug Indicator.

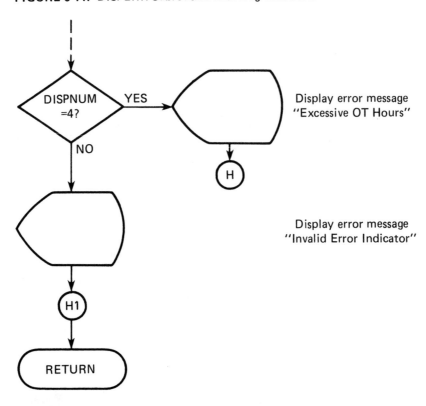

variable DISPNUM. (These messages should be included in both the extended description for Module 113 and in the flowchart for DISPERR.) Note that the fourth decision point takes into account the most common condition (no overtime) and jumps around that overtime processing to the connector K2. This eliminates unnecessary validity checking as well as the possibility of the program displaying an incorrect error message.

Flowcharting and IPOs

Throughout this chapter examples of the payroll problem have been used to illustrate flowcharting. In most cases, these flowcharts have provided a more detailed description of the actual logic that is implied in a structure diagram. Because flowcharting preceded IPOs in the evolution of program design tools, it became common to see flowchart symbols used in the IPO chart for program processes. Figures 6-14 and 6-15 show examples of this use.

FIGURE 6-12. "Hire That Person" Flowchart.

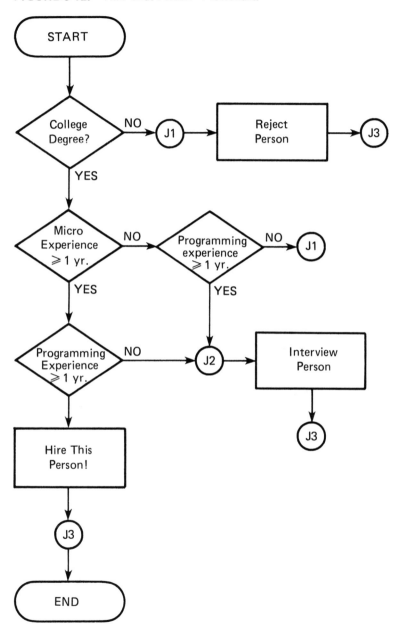

Strict rules of IPO development dictate the use of flowchart symbols only at the process, or detail, level. However, because these symbols can greatly aid you in visualizing the input and output of a

129

FIGURE 6-13. Payroll Problem Hours Validation.

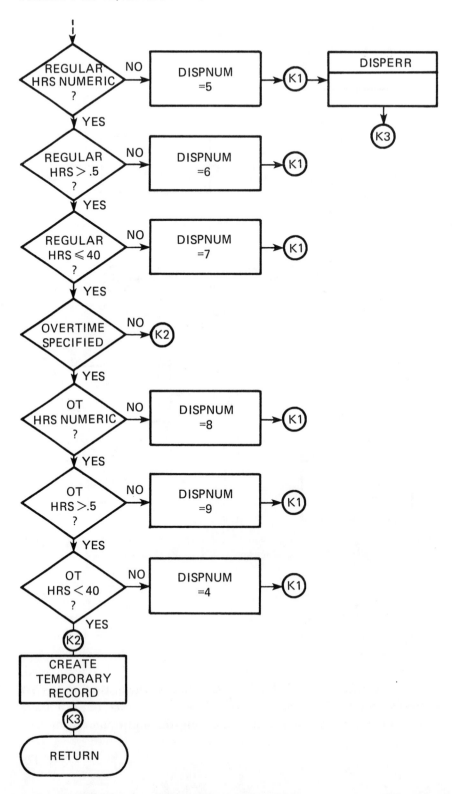

FIGURE 6-14. Flowchart Symbols in IPO Diagram.

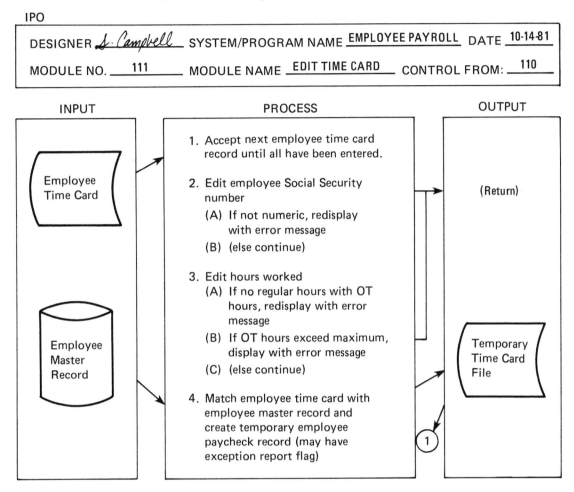

process, it is recommended that these symbols be used whenever possible. Be sure to refer to Appendix C for all those symbols available.

A Few Last Words

The symbols used in flowcharting help you visualize the detailed steps of your program logic. Initially, you will probably be inclined to draw a symbol for every line of program code you ultimately need to write. Although this ensures that every piece of logic is detailed, keeping such an involved piece of program documentation up-to-date is quite difficult. Indeed, the major drawback of program flowcharts is the difficulty encountered in keeping them current. A flowchart that does not accurately reflect program code not only is of little

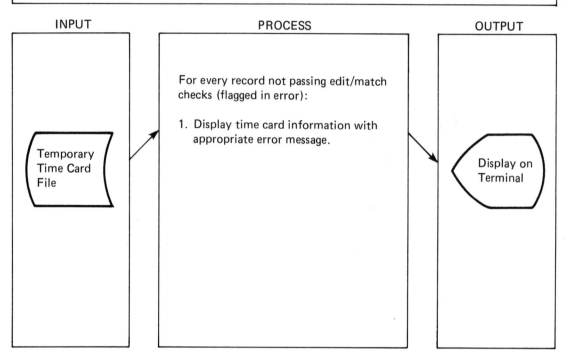

FIGURE 6-15. Flowchart Symbols in Input and Output Areas of IPOs.

use, but also can be downright frustrating. As with all other design tools, then, it is important that you modify the flowchart whenever you modify the logic of your program. If this is done with diligence, a program flowchart can remain a valuable documentation tool once its usefulness as a design tool is finished.

One way to ensure that your flowcharts will be easy to update is to place only one vertical flow on each page. Also, keep your continuation connector identifiers (A1, A2) in a consistent logical order. For example, you may choose to have the first two digits represent the page number and the last two digits represent the connector number on that page—for example, 0301, 0302. Whatever *convention* or style you choose, be consistent in its application.

CONCLUSION

Flowcharts are used to pictorially represent progressively greater detail of the flow or logic of a system or program. The pictures are derived from the use of flowchart symbols established by the American National Standards Institute (ANSI). These symbols are usually drawn with a template as a guide, although some of the symbols require additional lines to be drawn inside.

Where space permits, the activity represented by the flowchart symbol should be specified inside. Otherwise, the descriptive phrases should be written directly to the right of the respective symbol. (You may wish to associate this text with the appropriate flowchart symbol by using the annotation symbol.)

The general logic flow represented by the flowchart should be from the top of the page to the bottom. Only when absolutely necessary should flowchart symbols be added to the side of the main flow, and those should only appear to the right. The processing flow should be symbolized with lines and arrows (when necessary) between the symbols.

Subroutines should be flowcharted on separate pages. The entrance symbol should identify the name of the subroutine. As with program or module flowcharts, subroutines should have only one entrance and one exit (beginning and ending) point. In the main flowchart, calls to subroutines should be indicated by a process box with a horizontal stripe underlining the subroutine name.

Flowchart symbols can be arranged into three basic constructs: the process, the binary decision, and the loop. A special type of binary decision construct called case logic involves a string of binary decisions, each dependent upon the value of the same variable. Loop logic can be further defined as DOWHILE or DOUNTIL, depending on when the loop condition is checked. DOWHILE loops have the condition checked before the process; DOUNTIL loops check the condition afterwards.

Flowchart symbols can also be used in IPO charts. There, they help identify the source of input and the destination of output. While it is most common to find these symbols only used to help describe processor modules on a structure diagram, you may use them wherever they prove useful.

Finally, as with all other design aids, flowchart development is an iterative process. Implicit in this is the continual updating and modification of the program flowchart to reflect actual program logic. Without this accurate representation, the flowchart will soon lose its usefulness in terms of program documentation for future reference.

Pseudocode

7

Congratulations! You're more than halfway through the book. Now is the time for you to be certain you understand the concepts presented in the first six chapters. If you have questions, try reading the topical material one more time. If you still have questions or doubts, ask your instructor or a friend to help you. It's important that you have a firm grasp of the material so you won't find yourself muddling through the next two chapters.

Pseudocode is a hybrid between the English language and high-level (English-like) programming languages. For this reason, pseudocode is useful for expressing program logic at the design stage and for transforming that program logic into actual program-code statements. If this sounds simple, it is. You have already learned to express program logic symbolically in the form of flowcharts, so you can now revert back to sentences—pseudocode sentences.

In this chapter you will learn how to construct program logic in the place of flowchart symbols. This is done by using specific words intermixed with phrases representing flowchart processes. You will learn how to make the pseudocode more legible by using indentation conventions. Finally, you will also learn how pseudocode can be used in IPO diagrams.

RETURN TO WORDS

You will recall in developing structure diagrams that particular verbs held particular meanings. Pseudocode is similar because it relies on the use of specific words. However, the pseudocode *key words* represent logic constructs that were described in Chapter 6. The verbs and nouns used to express the process construct remain virtually unchanged. They still contain simple verbs and objects. However, pseudocode key words provide a consistent expression for loops and binary decisions. These key words are accentuated in pseudocode by printing them in capital letters, as opposed to the lower case letters used for the verbs and objects within the construct. To make this more clear, Figure 7-1 provides examples of a flowchart and the corresponding pseudocode for a process, a binary decision, and a loop construct for the shower routine.

You can see that the process construct contains no pseudocode key words. For a binary decision, four key words are used: *IF, THEN, ELSE,* and *ENDIF.* In pseudocode jargon, this construct is referred to as the *IF-THEN-ELSE* clause. The condition phrase (IF) always appears first, and is immediately followed by the action to be taken for a true condition (THEN). All of the statements, and there may be more than one, appearing after the key word THEN and before either the key word ELSE or ENDIF are performed each time the IF condition is determined to be true. Likewise, all of the statements appearing between the key words ELSE and ENDIF are performed each time the IF condition is determined to be false.

It is possible that the binary decision is used only to determine whether a process (or process string) should be executed. In this situation, it is assumed that the next pseudocode statement will be performed. Figure 7-2 shows this application. Here you would only wash your hair if it were dirty. However, you will wash your body regardless of whether you wash your hair. As you can see, the key word ENDIF is used to identify the point at which logic is no longer directly associated with the IF condition check. There must always be exactly one IF, THEN, and ENDIF for each binary decision construct. The ELSE clause should be included only if it is necessary.

The key words used in the loop construct should look familiar to you—DOWHILE and ENDDO. Remember that the DOWHILE loop construct involves checking for the condition before processing within the loop has been performed. Had this check been made after the loop processing, the key word DOUNTIL would have been used. Nonetheless, all processing between the DO and the ENDDO is performed each time the condition is positive. In the example shown in Figure 7-1, the hot and cold water adjustments will be performed while the water temperature is not comfortable for a shower.

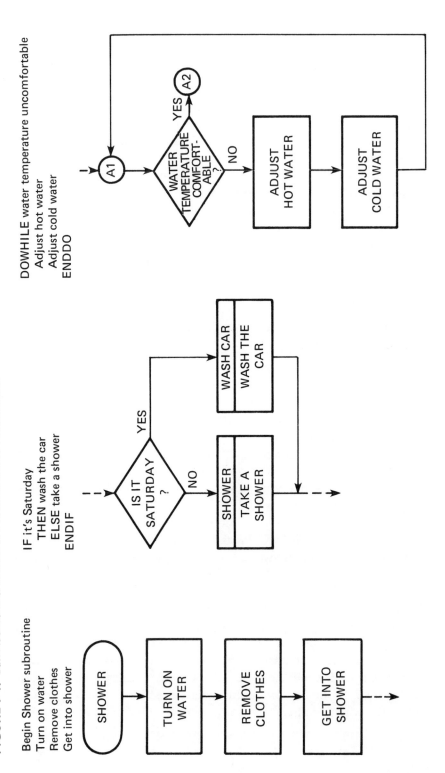

FIGURE 7-1. Basic Constructs Shown as Flowcharts and Pseudocode.

FIGURE 7-2. Assumed Action of False Condition.

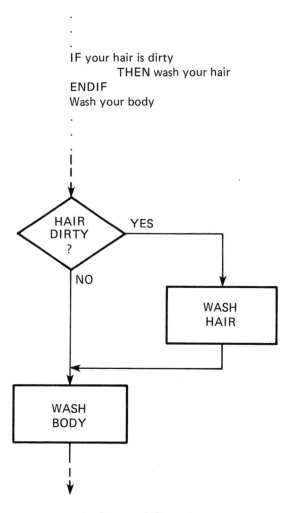

In Place of Flowcharts

The best way to illustrate the use of pseudocode in designing a program is by example. Refer back to Figure 6-8 and try writing out the pseudocode for each flowchart. Now refer to Figure 7-3 and compare your results. Did you remember to include the connectors as labels? You may notice that the loop construct for the accumulator method and the DOUNTIL types are the same. This is because in both cases the check for completion is performed after another record has been read.

In all three cases, note how the processes to be performed within the loops are indented. Such indentation helps you identify where

FIGURE 7-3. Pseudocode of Various Loop Types.

Set NUMEMP to zero	Read initial value of NUMEMP	Read initial value of NUMEMP
A1: DOUNTIL NUMEMP equals 12	A2: DOUNTIL all employee records are read	A3: DOWHILE there are more employee records
Read record	Read record	Read record
Increment NUMEMP	Decrement NUMEMP	Decrement NUMEMP
ENDDO	ENDDO	ENDDO
(Accumulator Method)	(DOUNTIL Loop)	(DOWHILE Loop)

a loop closing (ENDDO or ENDIF) statement is required. The key to understanding the logic implied in pseudocode loops is knowing where the logic continues at the end of the loop. In each case, processing will continue at the DOWHILE or DOUNTIL point so long as that condition prevails. Once the DO loop is completed, the logic flow will continue at the statement immediately following the ENDDO pseudocode statement (not shown in this example). In each case, also note how the ENDDO is aligned with its respective DO statement. This alignment correlates the particular ENDDO with the appropriate DO.

Now that you understand the basis of pseudocode, let's complicate matters just a bit. Refer back to Figure 6-9 and try writing the pseudocode for module INPTRX. Now compare your results with Figure 7-4.

You may have had some difficulty expressing the conditional (IF) clauses. Generally, it is best to test for the condition that would cause branching out (to the right) of the main flow stream. Sometimes this results in a negative test (for example, edit checks *not*

FIGURE 7-4. Pseudocode of INPTRX Subroutine.

```
           Begin module INPTRX
    C1:    Get input transaction record
           IF record different than last
               THEN  edit employee number
                     Edit employee hours
                     IF edit checks not okay
                         THEN call DISPERR subroutine
                              GOTO C1
                     ENDIF
               ELSE GOTO C2
           ENDIF
           Locate master record by calling LOCMREC subroutine
           IF master record not found
               THEN  call DISPERR subroutine
                     GOTO C1
           ENDIF
    C2:    Return from subroutine INPTRX call
```

okay) which then leads to a more logical flow of the pseudocode. In this case, the pseudocode was greatly simplified by making this negative check. Once the negative condition processing (call to DISPERR and return) was specified, the subroutine logic could be continued and, as such, no ELSE clause was necessary.

The pseudocode in this example is simplified because it does not contain any DO clauses. Instead, the conditional clauses are treated as independent binary decisions with processes terminated with *jumps* (GOTO's) back to the A1 statement. This logic is acceptable, although it is not wise to use GOTO statements. They tend to cause the reader to get lost!

If at all possible, you should not use GOTO statements. Rather, try substituting either DOWHILE or DOUNTIL clauses. Take another look at Figure 6-9 and look for the conditions that can be expressed by DO loops. Try rewriting your pseudocode for this example using one DOUNTIL and one DOWHILE loop without any GOTO statements. Now compare your results with Figure 7-5.

FIGURE 7-5. Pseudocode of INPTRX Subroutine with No Jumps.

```
Begin module INPTRX
DOUNTIL employee master record is matched or until input
        doesn't change
    Get input transaction
    DOUNTIL all edit checks passed
        Edit employee number
        Edit employee hours
        IF edit checks not okay
            THEN call DISPERR subroutine
                 get modified input transaction
        ENDIF
    ENDDO
    Locate employee master record by calling LOCMREC subroutine
    IF record not found
        THEN call DISPERR subroutine
        ELSE create employee payroll record
    ENDIF
ENDDO
Return from subroutine INPTRX call
```

Notice that the conditional clauses are still necessary for the DISPERR subroutine calls. However, once that condition is considered, the test for the DO loop is performed (remember that DOUNTILs perform the check after loop processing is completed). Only after the DO condition is satisfied does the logic continue to the statement following respective ENDDO. In Figure 7-5 an attempt to locate the employee master record will not be attempted until all edit checks have been passed with no errors.

Also notice in Figure 7-5 how the pseudocode is indented not only for each DO loop but also for each IF clause. The two DO loops provide an example of a special type of logic construct called nesting. The edit DOUNTIL loop is said to be *nested* within the matched record DOUNTIL loop. That is to say that the editing must first be checked and passed before the matching of the master record. However, if the appropriate master record cannot be found, processing will continue after displaying an error message by accepting another input transaction which itself must then pass edit checks.

Figure 6-10 provides another example of a flowchart construct that can more easily be expressed with pseudocode. Try your hand at translating this into pseudocode and see how closely yours resembles that in Figure 7-6. In this example, each conditional statement should be treated as discrete, or not part of a loop. Notice how in the flowchart the logic jumps to the end of the subroutine once a single condition is found to be true, and the appropriate message is displayed. The pseudocode has this jump implied through use of the nested IF clauses. Remember that either the THEN clause or the ELSE clause will be performed, not both. Thus, once a THEN clause is processed, the logic jumps to the corresponding ENDIF. In this case, once an ENDIF is performed, the next logical statement is an ENDIF, and so on. Since this is not an indication of a loop (that would be indicated by an ENDDO), nothing happens. The logic continues to step through the series of ENDIFs until the return is performed.

Now take a close look at the last nested IF clause. Note that the ELSE statement indicates to the program operator that an unknown error has occurred. This is known as an *idiot check* and serves as a when-all-else-fails condition. Here, if the variable DISPNUM does not equal 1, 2, 3, or 4, the type of error message to be displayed is unknown. However, if the logic did not include this idiot check, processing would return to the point immediately following the call to this subroutine without the operator knowing an erroneous call to

FIGURE 7-6. Pseudocode of DISPERR Subroutine.

```
Begin subroutine DISPERR
IF DISPNUM equals 1
   THEN display "Not on Master File"
   ELSE IF DISPNUM equals 2
        THEN display "SSN Not Numeric"
        ELSE IF DISPNUM equals 3
             THEN display "No Regular Hours"
             ELSE IF DISPNUM equals 4
                  THEN display "Excessive OT Hours"
                  ELSE IF DISPNUM greater than or equal to 5
                       THEN display "Unknown Error (DISPNUM= n), Stop Program"
                       ENDIF
                  ENDIF
             ENDIF
        ENDIF
ENDIF
Return from subroutine DISPERR.
```

DISPERR had been made. The lesson to be learned here is that this sort of situation is commonplace, especially during the debugging phase of program development. Idiot checks placed throughout your program logic will help you pinpoint logic errors much more rapidly. Displaying messages that indicate the area of logic where the error was detected is particularly useful.

Remember that in Chapter 6 the flowchart construct in Figure 6-10 was called a case construct. Indeed, case logic pseudocode greatly simplifies this string of nested IF clauses. Refer to Figure 7-7 for this example.

It's important to understand that in case logic the object of the condition check, in this example DISPNUM, can have only one of the values for each CASE process. Once processing for the appropriate case condition is performed, the logic jumps to the ENDCASE statement. Notice how the idiot check is the invalid CASE condition.

Pseudocode in IPO Diagrams

As flowchart symbols can be used in IPO diagrams, so can pseudocode. The pseudocode statements are written in the process portion of the IPO diagram in place of the verbiage. Figure 7-8 shows how this simplifies and abbreviates the verbiage necessary to describe what processing needs to occur in each program or module. In this example, providing a pseudocode description of the processing to be performed by the DISPLAY-UNMTCH-RECORD module (Figure 4-12) eliminates the need for the associated extended description shown in Figure 4-13.

FIGURE 7-7. Pseudocode of DISPERR Subroutine CASE Logic.

```
Begin subroutine DISPERR
CASE  ENTRY DISPNUM
        CASE 1 display "Not on Master File"
        CASE 2 display "SSN Not Numeric"
        CASE 3 display "No Regular Hours"
        CASE 4 display "Excessive OT Hours"
        CASE Invalid, display "Unknown Error (DISPERR= n),
                    Stop Program"
ENDCASE
Return from subroutine DISPERR call
```

FIGURE 7-8. Pseudocode in Process Portion of DISPLAY-UNMTCH-RECORD IPO.

```
CASE ENTRY DISPNUM
    CASE 1 display "Not on Master File"
    CASE 2 display "SSN Not Numeric"
    CASE 3 display "No Regular Hours"
    CASE 4 display "Excessive OT Hours"
    CASE Invalid, display "Unknown Error (DISPERR=n), Stop
    Program"
ENDCASE
```

A similar application of pseudocode within an IPO can be accomplished by inserting the pseudocode of the INPTRX subroutine (Figure 7-5) into the process portion of the EDIT-TIME-CARDS IPO shown in Figure 4-8. In this example, however, the extended description provided in Figure 4-9 should be retained to describe the values of the error numbers, as well as the other amplifying information.

SUMMARY

Pseudocode is a cross between English and high-level programming statements. Program logic is represented by combining the pseudocode keywords summarized in Figure 7-9 and simple English phrases. Each pseudocode clause has a beginning (IF, DO, or CASE) and a respective ending (ENDIF, ENDDO, ENDCASE). If clauses are wholly contained within another pseudocode clause they are said to be nested. All nested clauses should be appropriately indented to make pseudocode more legible. Whenever possible, direct branching, or jumping, (GOTO) should be avoided.

Pseudocode may be used in place of flowcharts. While pseudocode is easier to modify than flowcharts, flowcharts may provide a

FIGURE 7-9. Pseudocode Key Words and Indentation.

```
    IF              DOWHILE      DOUNTIL      CASE ENTRY
       THEN            ENDDO        ENDDO        ENCASE
       ELSE
    ENDIF
```

better visual representation of program logic. This is exemplified by Figures 6-9, 7-4, and 7-5. In IPO diagrams, pseudocode may simplify the verbiage required to describe the necessary program logic.

A final advantage of pseudocode is that it is particularly useful in bridging the gap between program logic represented in flowcharts or IPOs and actual program code. It allows you to concentrate on the arrangement of the program statements without having to concentrate on any particular program language syntax.

Data Definitions

8

Throughout this book references have been made to a variety of data items. Some of these items have been called flags, counters, variables, records, and files. While you probably have a good idea what each of these items does, you may not comprehend the characteristics of each. These characteristics include length, variable or constant values, record and file types, and file organizations. This chapter will explore data as they pertain to the payroll problem as it has been structured throughout the book.

In the paragraphs that follow, the terms *data item, data element,* and *data* will be used frequently. Generally speaking, the term data item refers to independent information such as indicators corresponding to error messages. Data elements typically refer to portions of related information, such as an employee's name on the employee master file. While the term data is used frequently in discussing program design and development, its singular version—datum—is seldom used. The equivalent of a datum would be a byte of information. Both a data item and a data element frequently contain many bytes, and as such should not be referred to as a datum.

Probably the most obvious use of variable data items is in the calculation of numeric values. *Variables* are uniquely named data items that have different values, depending on the values used to determine that value. Some variables may have only alphabetic information, but their values change as the program is executed. Variables may be used to indicate particular conditions. For example, your program may need to remember how many times a particular loop has been executed. You may employ a *counter* variable for this purpose. A counter may be incremented or decremented, depending on its designated use, as was shown in Figure 6-8.

Another example of a variable helping a program remember something is *flags*. As variable data items, flags usually indicate the existence or absence of particular conditions. It may be easier for you to visualize the use of flags if you think of cloth flags being used at the beach. On California shores, a green flag indicates that swimmers are allowed in the water, a checkered flag indicates surfing only, and a yellow flag means that there are rip tides. Thus, each flag—through a single color or pattern—provides a complete explanation of swimming conditions. In a similar fashion, a single character (alpha or numeric) with a particular value can tell your program a great deal. It can indicate that a data element did not pass an edit check or that overtime processing must be performed, for example. A word of caution when using flags—avoid using the same flag for dissimilar purposes throughout your program. This could cause problems, analogous to your indicating that swimming or surfing is allowed when at that point the flag is being interpreted to mean the beginning or ending of an auto race.

Constants are very similar to variables because they, too, tell a particular story. However, constants never change values during program execution. Their values, or contents, remain the same at all times. Frequently, constant values are preset in the program code, or are hard coded, and thus do not change once the program is compiled. An example of a constant value may be the name of the company using the payroll system. This constant, referred to in other program code as COMPANY-NAME, would be set to "ABC TRUCKING" or to "XYZ ANSWERING SERVICE," depending upon where the software had been installed. Then, whenever the program code needs the installation's name at the top of a report page, the program code would use the contents of COMPANY-NAME.

Each of these data items, flags, variables, and constants are referred to as *variables*. Flags and constants can be thought of as special uses of variables. All variables are assigned a specific, unique name that is referenced within the program logic. It should be noted that variables are discrete entities. Each is considered to have a particular value at any given time.

Tables and Arrays

Occasionally you may want to manipulate a list of like data items or data elements. Assume that the employee master records are stored in numeric order based on Social Security number. This order may not be appropriate for some reports that the payroll system is to generate. The list of employee names would have to be reordered to reflect an alphabetical order. The most obvious way to perform this sorting would be through successive examinations of the list of employee names. Consider the list in Figure 8-1, and notice how each name is associated with an item number. This list, when it is part of a program, can be considered as a single unit—the employee *table* or *array*. Suppose this array were named EMPL. To reference a particular item of the array, you would need to provide what is called a *subscript,* which usually takes the form of a number in parentheses following the array name. For example, EMPL (2) would indicate the second item in array EMPL, or Jon Spark. Because there is only one number following the array name, and only one item (employee name) is being referenced, this array is called a *one-dimensional array*.

What would you do if you also wanted to reference a variety of data items associated with each array item? Figure 8-2 shows how each data item can be held in three separate arrays. In each array, the data associated with each item number correlate with the individual employee. This method works well until you need to reorder any one array and you want to retain the association relative to items in other arrays. For example, if you were to alphabetize array EMPL, you would want Item 1 in arrays ESSN and EBRATE to reflect Della Adams' Social Security number and base rate, not Millicent Manning's.

Keeping track of such ordering across arrays is quite cumbersome. Instead, a *two-dimensional array* can be employed, as shown in Figure 8-3. The array EMPLDATA can now be sorted alphabetically, and the corresponding data will retain its proper association. The various data components are referenced by row and column number.

FIGURE 8-1. List of Employee Names.

ITEM NUMBER	EMPLOYEE NAME
1	Manning, Millicent
2	Spark, Jon
3	Kessing, Maxwell
4	Adams, Della
5	Chu, Ming

FIGURE 8-2. Employee Information Arrays.

EMPL ARRAY		ESSN ARRAY		EBRATE ARRAY	
Item	Employee Name	Item	Employee SSN	Item	Employee Base Rate
1	Manning, Millicent	1	826315682	1	396
2	Spark, Jon	2	446283225	2	564
3	Kessling, Maxwell	3	546023565	3	343
4	Adams, Della	4	103854779	4	481
5	Chu, Ming	5	735460031	5	507

Thus, EMPLDATA (2,3) references Jon Spark's base rate of pay. Likewise, EMPLDATA (4,2) references Row 4, Item 2, which is Della Adams' social security number, and so on.

Arrays can take on more than two dimensions, although this is rarely required. Tables or arrays are used within your program to manipulate data that are similar in content, and where relationships of data items must be retained. Next, let's look at the characteristics of these data contained either in variables or in arrays.

Data Item Attributes

Most programming languages require that you specify how long you expect your variables or data items to be. For example, does your counter need one or two bytes for a maximum value of 9 or 99 respectively? How many characters are to be reserved for the company name? Generally speaking, a flag will require only one character. This will allow for up to 36 conditions if all digits and letters are used.

FIGURE 8-3. EMPLDATA Two-Dimensional Array.

ITEM	DATA ITEMS		
	1	2	3
1	Manning, Millicent	826315682	396
2	Spark, Jon	446283225	564
3	Kessling, Maxwell	546023565	343
4	Adams, Della	103854779	481
5	Chu, Ming	735460031	507

Most often, the length of each variable is expressed in numbers of bytes. (Recall that a byte is roughly equivalent to one character position.) Be particularly careful of the length you assign to variables used for numeric tables. Be certain that enough bytes are reserved for plenty of carrying. for example, Figure 8-4 shows employee net pay amounts and the grand total. If editing characters ($,.) are ignored, the individual net amounts could be expressed in five bytes. The total net amount, however, would require six bytes.

You should also consider the effect of growth. In one case, much effort to modify the payroll example can be avoided by planning for larger net pay amounts. Considering inflation and promotions, it is likely that at least John Spark's net amount in a few years will need six bytes. Also, if employees are added to the payroll, the total net amount may exceed $9,999.99, thus requiring seven bytes without editing characters.

Lengths are also frequently required when specifying the data elements contained in a data file. A *data element* is a piece of data with a unique value associated with each occurrence. Figure 8-5 illustrates the characteristics of some of the data elements contained in the employee master file of the payroll example. Notice how editing character positions have been omitted from the birthdate, Social Security number, and rate of pay data elements. Storing this information without special characters, such as dollar signs, commas, periods, and hyphens can save lots of file storage space.

Data Elements, Records, and Files

Let's take a moment to clarify the terms data element, record, and file. It may help if you think of these as though they were physical items. For example, Figure 8-6 depicts a *data file* as a filing cabinet—

FIGURE 8-4. Sample Net Payroll Report.

ABC TRUCKING PAYROLL AS OF OCTOBER 24, 1982	
EMPLOYEE NAME	**NET AMOUNT**
Adams, Della	$343.65
Chu, Ming	501.32
Kessling, Maxwell	295.84
Manning, Millicent	410.23
Spark, Jon	678.49
TOTAL	$2,229.53

FIGURE 8-5. Employee Master File Record Description.

DATA ELEMENT NAME	ALPHA/NUMERIC	LENGTH
EMPLOYEE-NAME	A	20
EMPLOYEE-ADDR-1	A/N	30
EMPLOYEE-ADDR-2	A/N	30
BIRTHDATE	N	8
SSN	N	9
FED-WITHLD	A/N	3
BASE-RATE	N	4
OT-RATE	N	4
DEPT-NO	N	4

here containing employee information. When you open the drawers of this cabinet you'll most likely find manila folders—one for each employee, each containing the same information. If the information is carefully organized in the same fashion for each employee, these folders are analogous to records within a data file. The data *records* referenced in this chapter will be of fixed length and by definition will contain room for the same information in the same order for every occurrence of the record.

Next, if you examine one of these folders you will discover which pieces of information are contained therein. These discrete pieces of information, as shown in Figure 8-5, are called *data elements,* or fields, on the records. In most cases, the length of these data elements must always be the same. This is because the program expects each field to begin at a particular point on the record. For example, Figure 8-7 shows the beginning and ending byte positions within the record for the employee biographical-demographical (abbreviated *bio-demo*) information. Note that the second row of data elements is a continuation of the first, since it begins with Byte Number 51. Also note how the lengths of the fields correspond to the tabular description of the record given in Figure 8-5. Either method of describing the contents of a record is acceptable. The tabular description method allows you to specify other particulars of the field, for example, whether it is alpha or numeric. However, the pictorial representation method shown in Figure 8-7 may make it easier for you to visualize the actual lengths of the fields as well as their relative placement.

FIGURE 8-6. Employee Data File, Records, and Data Elements.

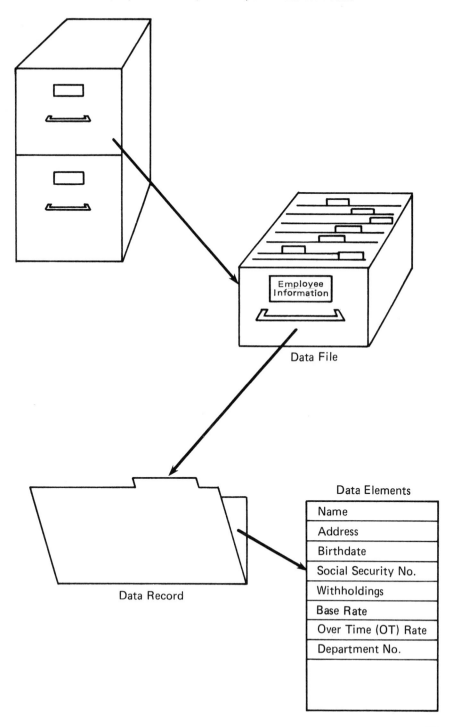

FIGURE 8-7. Employee Master File Record Layout.

EMPLOYEE NAME	EMPLOYEE ADDRESS-1
1 20	21 50

EMPLOYEE ADDRESS-2	BIRTHDATE	SSN	FED WTHLD
51 80	81 88	89 97	98 100

BASE RATE	OT RATE	DEPT NO
101 104	105 109	110 113

When designing records, it pays to place related fields together. Again, looking at Figure 8-7, notice how the employee's name and address are adjacent. If you are using the employee's Social Security number as an identification number, it should be placed at the beginning of the record. This facilitates accessing and sorting the records in numeric order. Another consideration in designing records is the possibility of expansion. Expansion can sometimes be predicted. With zip codes, for instance, long before the nine-digit zip code was actually in use, the general public was aware of the U.S. Postal Service's intention of expanding the five digit code. A wise program designer would have ensured that ample space was available on the employee bio-demo records to accommodate a full nine-digit code. Suppose the Employee Master File Records were in the design stages when the news of the nine-digit zip hit the streets. Figure 8-8 shows you some options for accommodating this news.

Option 1 is probably the best design solution if no records already exist. If they do, they must be converted to the new format so that fields following the original five-digit zip code are positionally adjusted five bytes further along in the record. Likewise, any program code must be adjusted so that data elements following the zip code will be properly interpreted.

Option 2 is totally unacceptable. In programming, we call this type of solution a *kluge* (pronounced kah-loo-ge). Never, never apply bandages to data designs or programs that make it difficult to keep track of the location of data or of the intent of particular processes.

FIGURE 8-8. Options for Accommodating Field Length Increase.

OPTION

EMPLOYEE ADDRESS-2	ZIP-1	ZIP-2	BIRTHDATE	SSN
51 80	81 85	86 89	90 97	98 106

OPTION 2

EMPLOYEE ADDRESS-2	ZIP-1	BIRTHDATE	SSN
51 80'	81 85	86 93	94 102

FED WTHLD	BASE RATE	OT RATE	DEPT NO	ZIP-2
103 105	106 109	110 103	104 107	108 111

OPTION 3

BASE RATE	OT RATE	DEPT NO	ZIP
101 104	105 109	110 113	114 122

If you forget where the other portion of the zip code resides, most likely anyone else trying to maintain or modify your code will find this sort of design frustrating.*

Option 3 is a compromise between the first two options. This scheme simply adds the new data element (all nine bytes) to the end of the record. The area formerly used for the five-digit zip code is then available for other uses. While this solves the accommodation problem for the larger zip code, it does not allow for all address data elements to reside together.

File Types

To alleviate any confusion between arrays and data files, think of arrays as being temporary storage areas within programs, and conse-

---

*Historically, some programmers have used these "innovative" approaches to make themselves indispensable to their employers. Indeed, many employers have had to suffer long hours of overtime to maintain such systems. It's wise for you to remember the old adage that as soon as a programmer has made him- or herself indispensable, get rid of that employee!

quently existing only within the processor memory. Data files, on the other hand, are collections of data that are stored or saved on auxiliary storage. As the name implies, data files contain only data on which your program can operate, and are organized by data elements (or fields) within records.

There are other types of files resident on microcomputer auxiliary storage media. The two most common are system files and program files. *System files* consist of the operating system and supporting utility object code. These files are supplied by the hardware or software manufacturer. *Program files* contain only program code, either in source or object form, which you create.

DATA FILE ACCESS METHODS

There are three basic ways in which data files can be organized—sequential, indexed sequential, and direct access. This section will introduce the characteristics of each file organization access method, including the physical file organization, efficiency of access, what is required to insert or delete records, and when its use is appropriate.

Sequential Access Method (SAM)

The simplest file organization is called *sequential*. Its name accurately reflects how the records appear on the file—one right after the other. The order in which the records appear is the order in which they should be processed. Thus, before a sequential file is created it should be organized in a desirable order for processing, for example, alphabetically or numerically. This is because each record in the file must be read to progress further into the file.

To better visualize this, examine Figure 8-9, which represents a portion of the data elements contained in the employee master file. The semicolon shown separating the data elements is not part of the file, it is only to improve legibility. Assume in all of the examples presented in this section that the data element used to identify a specific employee is the Social Security number. Also assume that the file was built in the order that the records were processed (randomly as the list in Figure 8-9 indicates).

Now suppose that the time cards are sorted in ascending (smallest to largest) numeric (SSN) order before they are to be matched with employee master-file records. In order to perform this match-

FIGURE 8-9. Sequential File Organization—Disorganized.

RECORD #	SSN; NAME
1	826315682; Manning, Millicent
2	446283225; Spark, Jon
3	546023565; Kessling, Maxwell
4	103854779; Adams, Della
5	735460031; Chu, Ming

ing, the first four records would have to be read and compared before the first SSN match could occur. Likewise, for the second time card, the file would again need to be examined from its beginning, resulting in the first two records having to be read, and so on. With sequential files, each record in the file must be processed since there is no way to jump to the appropriate record. Hence, sequential files should, if possible, be organized by a particular order based on a data element or *key*. In this case, the key would be the employee SSN. Figure 8-10 shows how this file would look if it were organized in this fashion.

While sequential files are easy to access (read a record, compare the search key field, read the next record, and so forth), they can be quite cumbersome to maintain. For example, suppose that employee Karl Geer (SSN 616-19-8947) was hired and needed to be added to the employee master file. The existing master file would need to be read and written to another location, record by record, before *and* after Karl Geer's record had been inserted. As there is no way to jump into a sequential file, there is no way to plug in new records.

FIGURE 8-10. Sequential File—Organized Numeric by SSN.

1	2	3	4	5

Record #	SSN; Name
1	103854779; Adams, Della
2	446283225; Spark, Jon
3	546023565; Kessling, Maxwell
4	735460031; Chu, Ming
5	826315682; Manning, Millicent

The entire file must be rewritten to accomplish additions. Deletions pose a similar problem. Each record on the file (except the first record) must be preceded by another record. Thus, no empty records will be found on sequential files. Because of the physical characteristics of the magnetic tape medium, and the method used by the hardware to physically locate the beginning of another record, it is not possible to read a tape file to a certain point and then delete a record or begin writing records. Rather, all records must be rewritten, omitting those records being deleted.

The sequential file organization (also called the sequential access method, or *SAM*) is the only type of organization available for magnetic tape. All disk media can contain SAM files. Figure 8-11 summarizes the features of SAM files.

Indexed Sequential Access Method (ISAM)

The *Index Sequential Access Method,* or *ISAM,* resolves many of the problems inherent with SAM files. Its primary characteristic is that an index or separate portion of the file containing key elements of the data records correlates a particular record with an approximate location on a direct access storage medium (diskette or disk). The index is organized sequentially, but only contains the key and the corresponding location. Figure 8-12 illustrates the sample employee master file. The index contains the employee Social Security numbers (the key) and the corresponding track number, which contains all of the employees' master file information.

You will also notice in Figure 8-12 how each track contains blank or empty records. This extra space is originally built into the file to provide room to add records. Furthermore (and not shown

FIGURE 8-11. Sequential (SAM) Characteristics.

Order:	One after another in order of processing.
Accessing:	Must read all preceding records, one at a time, until appropriate record is located.
Insertion:	Requires rewriting entire file.
Deletion:	Requires rewriting entire file.
Efficient:	Only when entire file needs to be processed in the order in which it is organized.
Advantage:	Can be used on any type of auxiliary storage medium.

FIGURE 8-12. Example of ISAM File.

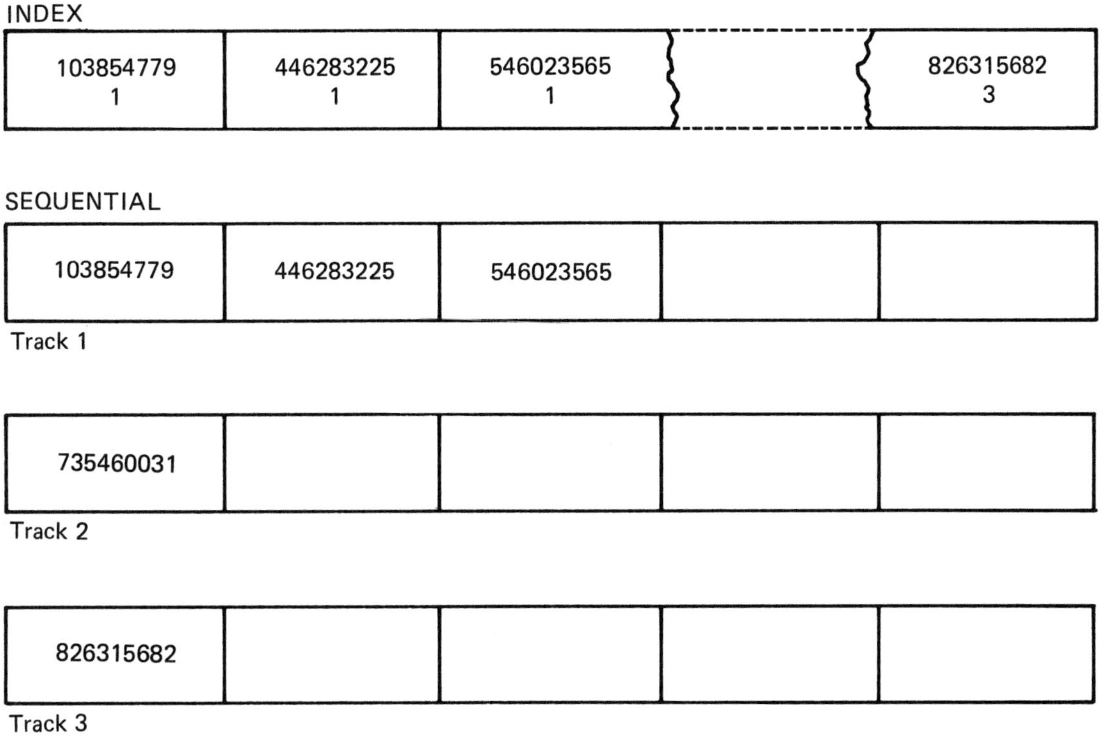

INDEX

103854779 1	446283225 1	546023565 1		826315682 3

SEQUENTIAL

103854779	446283225	546023565		

Track 1

735460031				

Track 2

826315682				

Track 3

here), spare tracks may be reserved to hold *overflow* resulting from a particular track filling up with information. The tracks originally designated to hold information are called *prime tracks,* and the additional reserved tracks are called *overflow tracks.* When an overflow track is used it becomes an extension of a primary track, as shown in Figure 8-13.

The real advantages of ISAM files become evident when records must be updated, added, or deleted sporadically. If a record is updated, only the record itself must be rewritten. When a record is added or deleted, the index must be rewritten from the point of change, and the affected track (and possibly the overflow track) must be rewritten. As you can imagine, with the index providing ready access to the data records, and with only one or two tracks in the file being affected, access to data records, and your ability to modify them, is much easier and faster. Figure 8-14 provides a summary of ISAM attributes.

FIGURE 8-13. ISAM Overflow Track Usage.

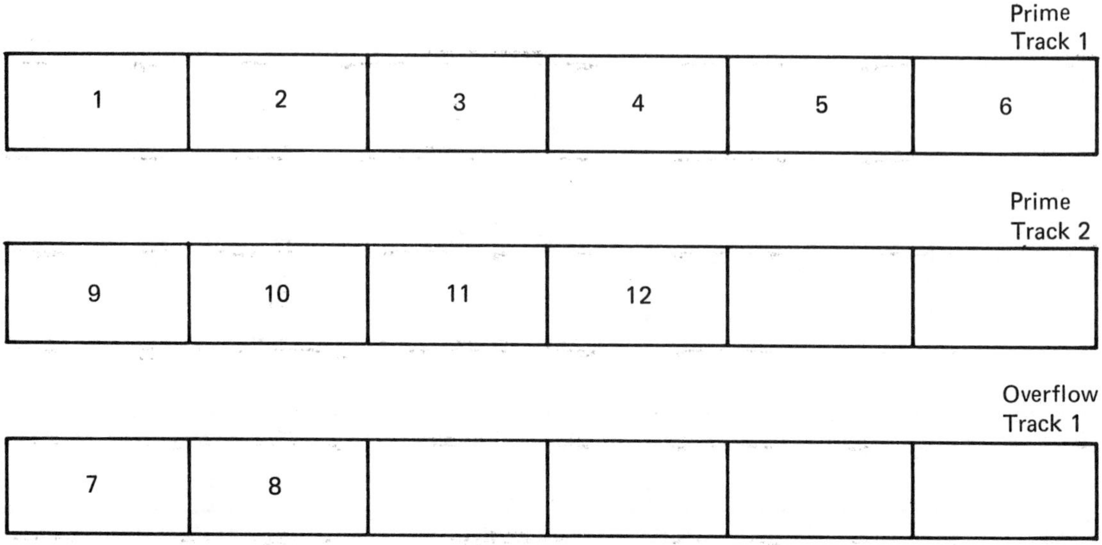

						Prime Track 1
1	2	3	4	5	6	

						Prime Track 2
9	10	11	12			

						Overflow Track 1
7	8					

Direct Access (DA) Method

The most sophisticated file organization (short of a data base management system, which will be discussed later) is the *Direct Access* (DA) method. With this method, the physical location on the disk is calculated from data elements on the record. For example, the Social Security number can be mathematically manipulated to calculate the *track* and *sector* number where the beginning of that record will be found. This eliminates the need for the program to read records and compare key values to locate the appropriate record. Figure 8-15 illustrates how a DA-formatted file might appear. Note how spaces are left for records 3, 6, 7, and 11. Those spaces in the file will only

FIGURE 8-14. Indexed Sequential Access Method (ISAM) Characteristics.

Order:	Index in sequential order by key. Data in sequential order by key with room for expansion.
Accessing:	More efficient than SAM because only index needs to be searched sequentially. After key found in index, access is direct.
Insertion & Deletion:	Requires rewriting only portions of the file.
Efficient:	When all records do not need to be processed.
Disadvantage:	Restricted to direct access storage media. Records must be fixed length.

FIGURE 8-15. Direct Access (DA) File Representation.

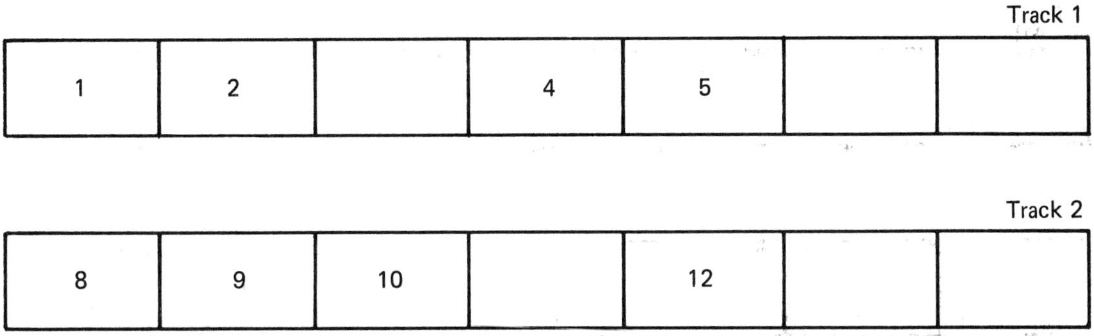

Track 1

1	2		4	5		

Track 2

8	9	10		12		

be filled when records containing data which, when mathematically manipulated, map to that location. The obvious benefit of DA files is extremely rapid access to individual records. However, DA files require more physical storage space to accommodate room for potential records (which may never exist). Thus, a disadvantage is wasted storage space. Also, if all records on the file must be processed, the mathematical calculations can become time-consuming in comparison to stepping through the file record-by-record. Figure 8-16 summarizes the attributes of a Direct Access organization.

As you can see, each access method has its strengths and weaknesses. If you only have a cassette tape auxiliary storage device, you needn't be concerned with the ISAM and DA organization methods. However, if you are going to keep your data files on diskette or hard disk, you will need to carefully consider which access method will best suit the needs of your application. It is always best to use the sequential method when you are beginning to design programs and

FIGURE 8-16. Direct Access (DA) Method Characteristics.

Order:	Random, based on manipulation method used on key data elements.
Accessing:	Very rapid once data elements are massaged to produce track/segment location.
Insertion & Deletion:	Only affect the individual record. Hence, rapid.
Efficient:	Only when individual records must be accessed in a random order, and space is not an issue.
Disadvantage:	Restricted to direct access storage media. Also, all possible key values must be anticipated which may result in excessive unused storage space.

data files. Once you have gained some experience with data manipulation, you can begin to experiment with the ISAM and DA methods, which are more advanced.

FILE SIZES

When working with microcomputers, it is very common to run out of auxiliary storage for your data. It cannot be stressed enough how important it is to accurately estimate what storage space your files will require. Experience has taught many programmers that it is better to guess on the high side. Certainly you can imagine how discouraging it would be to design, code, and test your program only to run out of storage space, and render your program useless.

File size estimation is not difficult. All that is required is for you to add up all the bytes contained in the data elements. This will give you the minimum size of each record. Then, multiply this times the *maximum* number of records you anticipate for that file. This will give you a nice big number, but not big enough. The operating system also needs some storage space to keep track of your files. Take your estimated file size and multiply it by 1.25. *Now* you have an estimation that will allow for everything you anticipate, plus some more.

Next, compare this number with the number of bytes contained on your storage medium. (Refer to Tables 1-1 and 1-2.) If your file requirements are too large for your storage medium, don't panic—all is not lost. Instead, you must become a bit more creative. Take a close look at your data elements. Can any of these be calculated each time the program is run, instead of saving them on file? Are all the data elements absolutely necessary? Can any of the elements be shortened or abbreviated? Can your file be segmented into smaller logical groupings? An example of how the employee master file could be shortened and segmented is shown in Figure 8-17. Note how the address fields have been shortened from their original length, as specified in Figure 8-5. Also, the zip-code field has been increased. It's important to understand that when such a file is split into multiple files, a common data element must be carried on all files. In this case, the employee Social Security number provides the common link to associate bio-demo and payroll information for individual employees.

FIGURE 8-17. Segmentation of Employee Master File into Employee Bio-Demo and Pay Information Files.

EMPL-BIO-DEMO			EMPL-PAY		
EMPLB-SSN	N	9	EMPLP-SSN	N	9
EMPL-ADDR-1	A/N	20	EMPL-FEDW	N	3
EMPL-ADDR-2	A/N	20	EMPL-BASER	N	4
EMPL-ZIP	N	9	EMPL-OTR	N	4
EMPL-DOB	N	8	EMPL-DEPT	N	4

Data Safety and Integrity

If you consider that the payroll program may only be part of a much larger system, the logical grouping of the information as shown in Figure 8-17 has even more merit. Other programs or sub-systems may now access the employee bio-demo file without having to access the payroll information. This helps to ensure that none of the actual payroll information will be available for other programs to potentially alter. Thus, the validity or accuracy of the data can be maintained. This is referred to as *data integrity*.

To ensure additional data security (against loss due to software or hardware failure), each of the data files should be copied, record-for-record, on a regular basis. This copying is called *backup*. Whenever a file is lost or destroyed (yes, it does happen), a backup copy can be used to *restore* the data file to its condition before the mishap occurred. Caution should be taken in blindly using your backup copy after your working copy fails. It is possible that the hardware, the disk drive, for example, is physically damaging the storage medium. If this were the case and you relied upon your backup copy, the odds are in favor of your backup file also being destroyed.

Data Bases

One last item deals with the subject of data bases. First, understand that data bases are data files on which the programs act. A data base can take the form of a SAM, ISAM, or DA organization. What has not yet been discussed are relations of data elements outside of the normal record association. Data Base Management Systems, or DBMSs, are software packages that with varying degrees of complexity and capability allow you to form relationships of data elements across the collection of data records.

There are many DBMS packages on the market today, each with its own strengths and weaknesses. What you must remember when you consider using a DBMS package is that in doing so you let that software package perform all file organizing and accessing. This may mean that unless you carefully consider how the data are to relate to one another you may be restricted at a later date. That is, some DBMS packages do not allow you to add data elements to your file once they have been defined and built. Also, most DBMS packages have maximum record lengths or maximum numbers of bytes in the file, which could also pose future restrictions.

Some of the most popular data base packages help you build hard-copy reports from that data. This is a wonderful tool, but may also restrict your flexibility. Because the files are structured to make the DBMS software efficient, it is quite possible that a program you write will not be able to access the data contained on that file. In summary, try to anticipate all your needs for your data before you select a DBMS package.

Building Your Data Design

One of the best ways to facilitate designing your files, and ensuring all data items are defined and used appropriately, is to begin your data design at the very beginning of your program design. Many programmers make a habit of keeping a notebook or a file of all data items, data elements, and file needs. This notebook should be organized into those three general categories. Each data element should correspond to all files in which it will be contained. Keep lists of all variables you plan to use, along with their anticipated use. Then, when you are flowcharting or pseudocoding, you will have a handy reference and can avoid using undefined variables or tables, or using multiple variables or tables for the same purpose.

Error Detection

9

You may be wondering why error detection is the topic of a chapter in a book on program design. It is because the different methods of detecting errors can be used to improve your design. Also, identifying and correcting errors in a program can never begin too soon. Even with the most basic problem definitions, *error detection,* or *debugging,* can be accomplished in a variety of ways. The different methods of locating and correcting problems will be discussed in this chapter and the next. This chapter will present methods for use primarily before you actually try to run, or execute, your program. Chapter 10 will discuss program testing in detail.

It has been said that designing and programming are inherently error-prone activities. Historically, locating and repairing program errors has proven to be both costly and time-consuming. It is generally accepted that approximately 50 percent of the effort expended on a program during its life cycle will be toward maintaining that program. Figure 9-1 represents the *life cycle,* or usefulness, of a program. As you can see, relatively little effort is spent actually coding the program. Significant effort, however, is devoted to solidifying the design, and to testing that design. The maintenance part of the pro-

FIGURE 9-1. Proportionate Effort During Program Life Cycle.

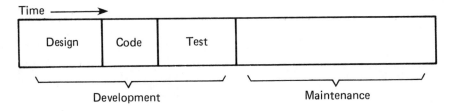

gram life cycle represents the repetition of a series of activities. These activities may be initiated by discovering additional bugs or by enhancing the original program. In either case, the activities are basically the same. They will be discussed in more detail in the next chapter.

Although program design is an error-prone activity, the vast majority of mistakes can and should be detected and corrected before any program testing takes place. The sooner bugs are caught, the easier it will be to correct them. Program execution is not the time to realize that a basic design flaw exists, for repairs will undoubtedly be very costly. Better to detect the error early so that repair will require a minimum of effort, and so that you will not feel defeated by your finding yourself starting over again from the beginning.

Errors can be grouped into two general categories: clerical and logical. Clerical errors are familiar to us all, and they usually take the form of typos, such as typing an r instead of a t. Other clerical errors include omitting punctuation marks, parentheses, or entire lines of code. Conversely, clerical errors may be the result of extra punctuation, parentheses, or entire lines of code being inserted.

Logical errors are typically more difficult to isolate. These errors may be the result of a lack of understanding as to what problem is to be solved, or the approach to the solution may have some flaws. Probably the most common logical error occurs when the program designer fails to take some situation into account ("I never *dreamed* that would happen!" or "Oops! I forgot to set that flag.")

Errors and Egos

Your attitude toward errors and error-detection can either help or hinder the quality of your final product. It is imperative that you separate your self-worth from the program's worth. You must be able to accept the fact that your program will have errors, and to encourage others to help you find these errors. The sooner you involve someone else in the error-detection process, the faster you will find and be able to correct the problems. It is important to *involve another person!* Someone asking a simple question may reinforce your understanding and approach or reveal an error.

At first you may feel embarrassed or threatened to have an outside party look at your program design or help you resolve a difficult situation. These feelings are natural because you are, in a sense, exposing how you think through a problem and find its solution.

Keep in mind that it is very rare for two people to develop the same solution. Instead of being embarrassed, look on that assistance as a learning experience. The following axioms may help you to overcome your ego involvement, both in seeking and giving error-detection assistance.

1. Everyone makes mistakes.
2. Everyone makes silly mistakes, and often these are repeated.
3. Everyone finds the mistakes of others more easily than their own.
4. There is no such thing as a stupid mistake as long as learning occurs.
5. Everyone loves having corrected an error, especially if finding the solution was a particularly frustrating experience.
6. The most elusive mistakes are usually silly and are frequently the simplest to correct.

Your understanding of the realities of error-detection is just as important as your attitude. As we've already established, *there will be errors*. Your goal should be to overcome this reality—to try to locate every little error as quickly as possible. If you approach error detection by thinking there are no errors to be found, that's precisely what will happen. You will find no errors—until later, when those bugs may come creeping out of the woodwork.

You should also understand that you may not be able to locate all of the bugs in your design or code. Aside from being impractical (time constraints, and so on), there may be other people using your program, and you can't possibly predict all the silly mistakes they may make in the process. Thus, they may reveal errors by virtue of a particular sequence of inputs or a particular combination of data that you had never considered.

Understand that the person who designs or codes the problem solution may read logic into a solution that, in reality, is not there. Have you ever read a sentence in a book twice, only to realize that the first time you read it you inserted a nonexistent word for one that was printed? The mind has a marvelous way of anticipating and believing that a particular fabrication is a reality. That is why it is so important for you to seek the assistance of a less-biased individual.

Error detection should be fun! After your preliminary personal review of the design and code, you should involve others and view this as an opportunity to enjoy yourself. Play detective! When you approach error detection positively (it's *good* to find errors, and you will find *many* of them ...), you'll find and resolve them during those stages when it's easiest to make repairs.

ERROR-DETECTION METHODS

Over the years, programmers have successfully employed five generic methods for detecting program design and code errors. They are: desk checking, design reviews, walkthroughs, compiling, and active testing. Figure 9-2 illustrates where in the design process each of these methods can most effectively be employed to isolate errors. As you can see, every phase in the development process can be checked with more than one method. Because each method has its strengths and weaknesses, it is wise to use more than one method whenever possible.

Each of these methods will be presented in the following discussion. In addition to identifying the respective strengths and weaknesses of each method, as summarized in Figure 9-3, the following questions will be answered.

1. What is the method?
2. How many other people should be involved?
3. What do these people need to do?
4. What do I need to do to employ this method?
5. How frequently should the method be used?

FIGURE 9-2. Applicable Error Detection Methods for Each Program Development Phase.

	DESK CHECKING	DESIGN REVIEWS	WALKTHROUGHS	COMPILING
Problem Definition	x	x		
Structure Diagrams	x	x	x	
HIPOs	x	x	x	
Decision Tables	x		x	
Flow Charts	x		x	
Pseudocode	x		x	
Data Definitions	x		x	x
Program Code	x		x	x

FIGURE 9-3. Strengths and Weaknesses of Various Error-Detection Methods.

METHOD	STRENGTH	WEAKNESS
Desk Checking	Simplest to do. Pertains to all phases of design process. Clerical error detection. Private, nonthreatening.	Mental set versus reality.
Design Reviews	Reaches many people.	Cumbersome to incorporate comments.
Walkthroughs	Quick, educational. Logical error detection.	Potential ego involvement.
Compiler	Syntax error detection.	Logic error detection.

Desk Checking

Figure 9-3 points out the importance of this method, the most basic of the four. Desk checking is simply the program designer or coder, sitting at a desk, plowing through the design looking for errors of omission or commission in either the design or code. It's very important that you double check your work before others review the design, or before you compile your code. How many moments of embarrassment could be saved if every programmer simply took a few minutes to peruse his or her work! And how many moments of confusion *you* could save your reviewers by correcting those obvious mistakes before their review.

Because no one else is involved in this process, it can be ineffective unless you play a few games. First, pretend that what you are about to review was written by a person you are responsible for training. This will ensure that you: a) approach the work as something *new,* and b) take a real interest in both the quantity and quality of the work. You must always remember to approach any design, or code, review with the challenge of finding lots of errors.

Next, pretend that you have been assigned a particular perspective. In other words, concentrate on only one aspect of what you're reviewing. Change that perspective each time you look over your work. For instance, look for errors in functionality, completeness, and grammar or syntax—each in a different check. And, take a break between reviews. When you sit down again, remind yourself that it's a new piece of work, and that your purpose for reviewing it has changed.

Another trick that works for many people is to pretend that they are participating in a walkthrough. Talk to yourself! Verbalization forces you to think more sequentially in addition to keeping your mind alert. (Just remember that if you are not working in a secluded location, keep your voice down!)

When you are reviewing your code for logic errors, only one game is certain to reap lots of errors. Pretend you are the computer. Set yourself up with sheets of paper having areas reserved for the values of all variables you'll need, as well as ample space for all files you'll be using. Start at the beginning of the module, or routine, and pretend that you know nothing other than the logic statements in front of you. As the value of a variable or data element changes, line out the old value, record the new value, and proceed to the next statement. If you have infinite loops or forget to initialize a counter, this method will help you isolate the problem.

Finally, whenever you discover an error, congratulate yourself. One of the main reasons that desk checking becomes boring is because there is no one with whom to share your successes. Also, working alone provides you with no competitive stimulation to locate your own bugs before your peers find them. So, compete with yourself and give yourself a pat on the back every time you detect another error.

Design Reviews

One of the best methods for involving others and not feeling threatened is to utilize design reviews. Each individual participating receives a copy of your written design and is asked to evaluate its contents in private. The number of people providing these comments can vary from one to many, and it usually corresponds to the degree of formality. An informal review may involve a few of your peers. However, a formal review typically involves 10 to 20 individuals. In the work environment, the formal review would be conducted to ensure that the capabilities desired by the ultimate users of the program would be provided. Specifically, design reviews usually involve screen formats, report formats, and general flow requirements of the screens or programs to elicit the desired results.

QUALITY ASSURANCE

Because so many copies of the document are distributed for review at one time, it is helpful for you to keep a log of the reviewers of the document, whether their approval signature is required, and when the individuals actually returned their comments. Figure 9-4 suggests a format and provides an example of a formal design-review log.

FIGURE 9-4. Sample of a Formal Design Review Log.

PROJECT NAME/ID: Payroll System

FORMAL DESIGN REVIEW OF: Screen formats Exception and Management Report formats

DATE SENT: 11-16-82   EXPECTED RETURN DATE: 11-30-82

	Name	Dept.	Sign. Req'd	Date Returned
1	June Hildegard	Person.	yes	
2	Max Bentley	Payroll	yes	
3	Jon Warren	Finance	yes	11-23-82
4	Mildred Sole	Inour.	no	
5	Kimmy Li	DP	no	11-21-82
6	Jeff Juarez	DP	no	
7	Lois McDonald	DP	no	
8	Merry Thomas	VP	yes	
9				
10				
11				
12				

The participants in a formal review are frequently asked to sign off on the design. This formality is desirable for two reasons. First, the signature certifies that the individual has, in fact, reviewed the document. Second, it signifies that the user finds the design acceptable. Although eetro-specing* is practically inevitable, at least there is documented proof that the user thought that he or she wanted the program in a certain way.

The most effective design reviews are those where each reviewer is asked to evaluate the document from a specific perspective. For example, one person may be asked to evaluate the design for completeness. Other individuals may be asked to pay particular attention to flexibility, maintainability, or compatibility. You should attempt to have only one perspective assigned to an individual. A cover letter briefly soliciting the reviewer's written comments by a certain date should accompany the document to be reviewed. This structures the process so that time will not be wasted either through duplication of effort or unnecessary delays.

Ideally, design reviews should only occur once. However, if many comments are received, you should attempt to address these and any questions either by modifying the design or by justifying why the design wasn't changed. In either case, all original reviewers should have the opportunity to review the design after modifications have been made. Sometimes subsequent reviews elicit additional comments and questions. This cycle can be stopped at any time, but should continue until unanimous user agreement is reached in a formal design review process.

Walkthroughs

Whereas design reviews tend to be somewhat impersonal, involving written communication, walkthroughs involve meetings with active participants. The idea of a walkthrough is generally credited to Gerald Weinberg in his book *The Psychology of Computer Programming.*** However, the structure and operation of formal walkthroughs is thoroughly addressed in Edward Yourdan's book, *Structured Walk-*

---

*Combination of the words retrospective and specification, meaning to change the original design specification after the program is developed. From experience, retro-specing is a phenomenon that undoubtedly occurs just when you think the project is completed. It's that one last little modification (also known as a *tweek*) that will improve the program by 50 percent to 100 percent. These are usually prompted by the user, once he or she has had a chance to play with the completed product.

**The Psychology of Computer Programming. (New York: Van Nostrand Reinhold Company), 1971.

throughs.* This highly detailed description of walkthroughs primarily pertains to very large programming projects where hundreds of programmers working in teams may be developing a single system. Since probably few of you will work in such an environment, this discussion will emphasize less-formal walkthroughs.

A walkthrough is a step-by-step, or sequential, review of your program design. This review takes the form of a discussion, with at least one other peer, of what the design actually does. You assume the role of the presenter, describe the details of what is being reviewed, and solicit constructive criticism. (This is when it is imperative for you to separate yourself from your creations!)

When selecting the participants, keep in mind that the goal of error detection is to locate and resolve as many errors as possible in the shortest period of time possible. You can help them to be effective by always seeking "walkers" who have an interest in what you are doing. This may include people who are helping you to design your program, or those who want to learn from you. (I maintain that the best test of your understanding of a problem or a solution is whether you can easily describe it, or teach it, to someone else.) If you are lucky enough to have a more experienced individual also interested, by all means enlist his or her help.

When you have compiled a list of participants, check to ensure that you have at least one and no more than seven people involved. These people should all be willing to invest their time to help you improve your program design.

Since walkthroughs do take time, it is wise to make this time highly productive. As with design reviews, each participant should be asked to review the material from a particular perspective. You can keep the walkthrough on a positive note by asking each participant to bring to the meeting at least one positive comment for every negative criticism. The meeting itself should be kept as brief as possible. Try not to spend time discussing grammar, for example. Instead, discuss those areas of logic where two heads are better than one. And, as with any meeting, record all comments. Keep those written accounts of decisions and major suggestions. One of the greatest time-wasters is trying to reconstruct the discussion that led to a particular decision (for example, why did we decide to put the employee's birth date on the employee master file instead of the employee retirement file?).

**Structured Walkthroughs.* (Englewood Cliffs, New Jersey: Prentice-Hall, Inc.), 1979.

If walkthroughs are held frequently, each meeting can be confined to an ideal length of about thirty minutes. Even if you have not reached your goal for content, if the meeting has continued for more than two hours it may be wise to adjourn, since your participants may begin to watch the clock more closely than they watch the program design in front of them!

Whenever you end a meeting, always remember to thank those involved for their time and candor. Let them know that you appreciate their help. When they leave, write down what is to be changed as a result of your walkthrough and *why* the change is to be made. This quick and simple procedure provides a development history that can be referenced weeks or months hence when you or your colleagues begin to doubt that the proper design decision has been made. Keep this recollection of the meeting in a project-development notebook.

After the walkthrough, you should try to incorporate as many comments into your design as possible, as soon as possible. This freshness of thought will help you to recall comments or ideas that may not have been written down. Once you have finished these modifications, recheck the new design for obvious errors, do a little more original work, and prepare for the next walkthrough. This cycle of review-correct-create-review provides a framework for constant progress, since you always add something new to what has been reviewed. Your participants will also welcome seeing new material with each walkthrough session.

The frequency of walkthroughs may depend on a variety of external factors, such as when participants are available for a meeting, when the program design is scheduled for completion, how much time you are able to devote to developing the design, and so on. There is no prescribed frequency for walkthroughs, other than to hold them as often as necessary—but only if they are productive and don't consume an excessive amount of time.

Perhaps more critical than the frequency of walkthroughs is when to begin holding them. The answer to this is very subjective and not easily found. Try not to hold a walkthrough (except perhaps with one other person) *too* early in the design process. Participants will not be able to grasp what your design is intended to do or how you are approaching the solution. Conversely, don't wait so long that the participants must muddle their way through enormous detail in order to grasp the general design.

Compiling

So, you've created your program design, held multiple reviews, corrected your design and coded the program. Great! Have you checked your code, both for clerical and logical errors? If not, be sure to do so. Woe to the programmer who uses the compiler for desk-checking. Compiling your program will only reveal errors in syntax and spelling, and only if a referenced variable is undefined will compilers notify you of an omission. This method of error detection does nothing to help you locate errors in logic. For this reason, compiling should be prefaced with plenty of design reviews, walkthroughs and desk-checking. (Remember that languages which are interpretive—translated to machine code as the program is executed—cannot be compiled.)

Your goal in using the compiler for error detection should be to obtain a clean, bug-free compile on the third try. Ideally, you should only have to compile your program once, and that will be without errors. Part of the rationale for eliminating errors before you compile has to do with the nature of compilers. To them, bugs are terribly prolific. There will be times, as many programmers will attest, when a 30-line program will generate 34 diagnostic errors. The only explanation for the errors may be a simple spelling error—an error that may be overlooked by many reviewers.

So compilers are very useful for syntax errors. Some are sufficiently complex as to understand when the compilation should abort (terminate abnormally). These sophisticated compilers usually issue two levels of error diagnostics: warning and fatal. Warning compiler errors may originate, for example, when your code attempts to move a 6-byte variable into a 5-byte field. Since the actual value being moved may in fact be only 3 bytes in length, the compiler calls your attention to the potential loss of data.

Fatal compiler errors occur when the logic of the compiler program cannot translate the coded instruction into a meaningful machine language instruction. The best example of this is attempting to divide by zero in a mathematical equation. When fatal errors occur that are not obvious to the designer, you may need to solicit the assistance of a more experienced individual.

Before seeking the help of anyone for understanding why your compile blew up, or generated errors, try to understand the explanations of the available diagnostic messages. Use your own gray matter when reading those manuals. If at first you don't understand, perhaps that diagnostic explanation will make more sense after you have sought help. Regardless, it is important that you read your manual *before* you seek help.

SUMMARY

Errors in program design and code are of two types: clerical and logical. Logic errors are usually the most elusive. Seldom does a line number begin flashing at you while you are desk-checking and say, "On this line, variable XYZ should have been set to 3, not 6." Many logic errors can be detected with the same tools used to locate clerical errors. Figure 9-5 summarizes the error-detection tools discussed in this chapter.

The least poular and singularly most effective method for detecting errors is desk-checking. Although this method may be a cure for insomnia, desk-checking at all phases of the development process is necessary to ensure that whatever is to be reviewed by others is reasonably accurate.

In order to locate more design problems, comments from other individuals can be solicited. Their comments may be written, as in a formal design review, or can be verbal in a walkthrough. User approval of inputs like screen formats, and outputs, like report formats, can be formalized by securing the representative signatures necessary. This formal sign off usually occurs after those individuals have convinced themselves that what they have seen in the design documents is what they actually want.

Walkthroughs can take on a very formal air. However, they may also be very brief and involve only two people. Their success is dependent on the participants' ability to criticize and question the item being reviewed (for example, HIPOs or data definitions) instead of criticizing the creator. Design changes should be documented for historical purposes. This documentation may take the form of meeting minutes. These minutes may also reflect approval of the users, provided that those users are actively participating in the walkthrough process.

The last error-detection method discussed was the compiler. Errors in syntax identified by the compiler should be the last errors you locate before actual testing. Before you compile your program, ensure that as many errors as possible have been detected and corrected. And before you begin to actually test your program, read the next chapter!

FIGURE 9-5. Summary of Error-Detection Method Characteristics.

METHOD	BRIEF DESCRIPTION	# PEOPLE	THEIR TASKS	YOUR TASKS	FREQUENCY
Desk Checking	Read, play computer	1	—	Maintain objectivity. Correct errors detected	Constant, ongoing, iterative. Always before others see your work
Design Reviews	Read through	Any number, varies	Review, provide written comments by certain date	Incorporate written comments and answer questions	Until approval signatures acquired on final pass
Walkthroughs	Step-by-step group evaluation and discussion	2-8	Preview material and comment from assigned perspective in meeting	Address all points made by others either by incorporating comments or by explaining	Once per week to two weeks
Compiling	Let compiler identify syntax errors	1	—	Correct errors indicated	Only three times per module!

Testing 10

Your program code should be in reasonably good shape now that you have completed preliminary error detection. Program testing should only be performed *after* you have performed design reviews, walkthroughs, desk-checking of code, and cleanup of compiler errors. However, there's much more to testing than performing tests. Preparation for testing should begin shortly after your design is solidified, or at least concurrent with your coding. This chapter will introduce you to the philosophy of testing, give you an overview of what testing involves, explain how to plan, prepare, and perform comprehensive testing, and describe what should be done after you have completed portions of the test. Finally, this chapter will close with a few general words of encouragement regarding testing and error correction.

Testing is the exercising or executing of your code in an organized and progressive fashion. It makes no difference if the code you're testing is newly designed, modified, or something that has already been tested. When you discover the code does not perform the steps in the program logic as you had planned, you have a *bug*. Bugs can be nasty, prolific things, and they are often difficult to isolate because they may manifest themselves only under particular sets of circumstances.

Debugging is the art of isolating and ridding your program of these problems. Programmers have tried over the years to display their debugging ingenuity by employing a variety of tools and techniques. Testing is, in itself, one of the techniques used in this debugging process. Figure 10-1 illustrates the application of testing during the error resolution cycle—a procedure similar to that of testing a brand new program. Because of this similarity, this chapter will concentrate on the new program perspective.

The importance of testing a new program may become more obvious if you draw analogies with common objects around you. For example, would you want to drive the first car of a new series if it had not already undergone extensive quality-assurance testing to ensure that it would start, accelerate, steer, and brake properly? Certainly you would not expect the space shuttle Columbia to have been launched the first time if its computers hadn't been proved to be reliable. Likewise, you should never attempt to implement any of your programs without first testing them thoroughly. You must at least ensure that your program solution actually does what the problem definition called for, and that it will perform as you anticipate.

Evaluating the reliability of your program under all anticipated conditions helps you assure the quality of the program. It is important to remember that this assurance should take the form of *re*assurance when you have modified the original code. This repetition is necessary if you wish to evaluate the impact those modifications may have had on areas of the program that have not been changed. The process of repetitive testing is a simple one, especially if the same test script is available each time you need to reestablish program quality assurance.

It should be clear that there is no such thing as too much testing. After all, how many computer failures have you encountered at the bank, department store, or airline counter? Usually, these problems are software-related. Therefore, it's not the computer's fault

FIGURE 10-1. Testing as Part of Debugging Process.

ERROR RESOLUTION STEPS	WHEN TESTING PERFORMED
Error noted	
Error reproduced	x
Error isolated	x
Error repaired	
Repair evaluated	x

that you were billed incorrectly. Instead, a special set of data and circumstances was presented in the program that had an impact on your particular case. The bugs responsible for the error might have been identified had more testing been performed on the program prior to its implementation.

This raises the question of how much testing is really necessary. The answer is that a program should be tested until the programmer and the user are satisfied that it will work reliably, under both expected and unexpected conditions. That is, the program should be tested until it can be demonstrated to work properly on any set or combination of data repeatedly. More objective limitations for testing can be defined by the unique constraints of time and resources (equipment, people, money), and testing will usually proceed until one of the resources (usually money) runs out.

Resource limitation is the cause of one problem inherent in most testing environments—it is simply not possible to test everything in a program. For this reason, it is wise to use your testing time efficiently and effectively. To be effective, it is best to involve others in the testing process. This will help you to overcome the second problem inherent to testing—programmer subjectivity. When you code a program, you develop a mental set about what it is to look like. You, therefore, will be less likely to detect omissions or unforeseen combinations.

The third problem to be overcome in testing is that of error avalanche—a situation where the resolution of one error may cause an onslaught of other seemingly unrelated errors. Programmers have often said, "I don't understand what could have gone wrong! I didn't change anything." Careful questioning will frequently reveal that, indeed, something was changed, but in another "unrelated" area. Never assume that the solution of one problem guarantees that all tests performed up to that point are still valid. The mission of testing is to find all problems and to never assume that an error is trivial and not in need of correction. There is no such thing as an insignificant error!

OVERVIEW OF TESTING

Take a moment to examine who is involved in testing and what these individuals are intended to do. As you may have guessed, those involved in testing include yourself and at least one other person. It is widely accepted that the more you involve the ultimate users of the program in testing, the more likely it is they will be satisfied with the end result. You should never be embarrassed if other people find bugs in your code. Instead, consider yourself fortunate to have the services of someone so observant. This assistance in pre-delivery testing will allow you to experiment without fearing destruction of "live data," as opposed to test data, and will provide you with a second viewpoint that can only help to point out where the program can be improved.

Those assisting you in testing should become involved very early in the process. Even before you begin coding, you should plan how you propose to test your program. While you are using the IPO and decision-table tools, collect your thoughts and compose a readable, well-organized test plan. Have those who will be helping you review these plans to ensure that your testing will be comprehensive. If the users of your program become involved at this early stage, they will be able to judge whether the program will be comprehensive and will produce the product they need. Later the users should actually perform the testing to guarantee that the program will meet their expectations.

Your involvement in testing is, then, more than simply exercising the program code. You must first adopt the proper attitude toward the testing process. Think of it as a demolition derby. Be aware that the more problems you find before the program is implemented by the user, the fewer problems someone else is going to discover. This positive attitude of actively seeking errors will increase the odds of your delivering a trouble-free product.

A proper attitude will also encourage others to help you test your program. It's essential that you detach yourself from the quality of your program. Be thankful that others are willing to help you shake down your program. No one will want to be part of this process if they expect to receive a negative reaction whenever they discover a bug. Encourage them to find new errors. You might even want to turn the whole process into a game. But above all, approach testing positively so that the entire experience is a pleasant, worthwhile, and educational one.

The educational aspect of testing cannot be ignored. Not only are your helpers learning how to use your program, but by properly planning and documenting your testing procedures you are developing training aids. A new user will be able to take your test plans and procedures, and learn how to use the program. Further, you will learn a great deal about your own program while you test and debug it. The very fact that you are looking for problem areas forces you to view the code differently. That different perspective will lead to a better understanding of your own logic, and that in itself can be quite an education!

Aside from acquiring the proper attitude toward testing, involving others in the process, and documenting the test results, you must do four things: plan, prepare, perform, and post-handle. These four tasks can be grouped into three phases of testing as follows:

Phase	Task
Before	Plan and prepare
During	Perform
After	Post-handle

These three phases are repeated every time you sit down at the computer to perform a test. Following these three phases will ensure that each test session will be efficient. The remainder of this chapter concentrates on these three phases.

PLANNING FOR TESTING

Remember that it is wise to begin planning for testing long before you actually begin the process. These test plans should incorporate three factors: objectives, organization, and attributes.

Testing Objectives

There are two primary objectives in testing, checking the reliability of the program and integrating, or fitting together, the pieces of the program. With your first few programming projects, you will probably be most concerned with your program's reliability. You will want to ensure that the program will operate reliably and accurately, regardless of the input data and the number of times the program is executed. For this reason, you will want to demonstrate that the functional components of your program work as they have been designed to under all possible conditions.

Reliability testing involves stress and endurance testing. Stress testing is important to ensure that the program can accommodate the rigors of data inaccuracies, as well as volumes. It is very important that you consider what your program will do when it repeatedly receives bad data, or when it cannot write anything more into a file, for example. Endurance testing is just what its name implies. It demonstrates how long the program will operate accurately. This is not important unless you are designing a program that must operate continuously and accurately over an extended period of time—for example, three days. In preparation for space shuttle flights, for example, it was imperative that the computer flight systems not only function properly for a single orbit, but also function properly over many consecutive orbits.

Integration is the second objective of testing. In your first few programs you may not need to perform integration testing because you will probably code your entire program at one time. However, as your programs become longer, you will want to code and test parts of the program separately. Referring back to the functional units concept discussed in Chapter 3, it may be easier for you to concentrate on fully developing one functional unit at a time. Integration of these functional units requires testing so that individual pieces, or functions, fit together properly. If, for example, flags are set in one functional unit, you will need to check the other units to ascertain that the flag is properly interpreted. If your program or system has been coded in functional units or modules, each piece can be tested independently for correct performance and accuracy. Only after the various modules have been integrated should stress or endurance testing be performed.

Testing Organization

Establishing an organization or approach for your testing is the second characteristic of your test plan. The importance of testing organization is proportional to the complexity of the program. Little organization of testing may be required to adequately exercise a program that would accept names and addresses as input and produce mailing labels for output. However, if the program is as complex as the payroll example outlined in this book, it behooves you to establish a logical sequence for testing the component parts. There are four general approaches to testing organization: the overconfident approach, the evolutionary approach, the top-down approach and the bottom-up approach.

The overconfident approach is analogous to a lack of organized testing. That is, all of the component parts are thrown together and testing begins. This is usually disastrous, no matter how confident you are of your coding. Because there is no tested base, it is very difficult to determine what caused any errors. It is much easier to isolate problems if you approach your testing one step at a time. Assure yourself that at least the basic units are reliable before you add unknowns or new components. The other three testing organization approaches use this building block philosophy.

Probably the most commonly used organization is the evolutionary approach. This involves coding the basic structure of your program, testing that structure, adding some more coding, testing all that you have completed so far, adding some more code, and so on. The program grows only as the reliability testing of the new base is completed. In the payroll example, this evolutionary process may begin with only the control modules being tested. To this base, the coding for Edit Time Cards could be added and tested. Then, when the coding to Create Employee Payroll Records is added, the control module and the edit process are tested in conjunction with the newly added code. Once each of these have passed reliability tests, you would have a base to which the Display Error Message code could be added. As you can see, the new code is most likely to be the source of errors should the base code no longer pass its reliability tests. Confining the amount of new code introduced in the testing sequence facilitates the isolation and detection of programming or logic errors.

Larger programs or systems may have more than one person involved in coding. The last two organizational approaches (special kinds of evolutionary approaches) are most applicable to these larger efforts. In the case of top-down testing, the control module is coded and tested first. Next, subordinate control functions are added to the base, and these are tested together. Calls to subordinate functions or processes are effectively ignored by inserting *dummy modules* into the program. Dummy modules consist only of an entrance and an exit, and are used to allow clean compiles. Later, as that processing level is added to the base, only the logic for that functional unit needs to be inserted. The major disadvantage to this scheme is that the individual processes are not tested until the very end. In a large system it may be more time-efficient to perform reliability testing on those separate components.

The last organizational approach, bottom-up, allows for such parallel testing. Just the opposite of top-down, bottom-up testing provides for all the independent processes to be coded and tested simultaneously. Once all these have passed reliability testing, their control functions are added. These functional units are then tested before they are integrated by the coding and testing of the next higher control functions. Implicit in this approach is that the core of the functional units have already been tested. The major disadvantage of this approach is that the program itself cannot be exercised until all cores are integrated into the whole.

Testing Attributes

In planning for testing, you should always consider the last factor—attributes. Novice testers are always good at planning tests that introduce data that are expected. However, good test plans—"good" implies the test will reveal the most bugs—will consider data that are not expected. Your test plans should state that you intend to test for both positive (expected) and negative (unexpected) conditions. This can be indicated by delineating tolerable limits for variable values and minimal functionality requirements of the program. In addition to negative and positive testing, another attribute of good test planning is repetition. Simply because something used to work is no reason to assume that the same portion of the program will continue to work after errors have been corrected. Always plan portions of your test that can easily be repeated periodically.

The final and most important testing attribute is documentation. It is imperative that you write down your test plan, your test procedures, the results of the test, what you accomplished, and what you plan to accomplish in the next test session. This documentation should be kept in order (usually chronologically) in a separate file. The time and energy you save investigating what happened the last time the test was performed will more than compensate for your original documentation efforts. Also, this testing documentation can provide the backbone for user documentation which will be discussed in the next chapter.

PREPARING FOR TESTING

Test procedures are the result of your thoroughly preparing for the testing process before it begins. Whereas your test plans outline generic items that need to be tested, the test procedures specify very clearly what should be done in order to accomplish the testing. These steps should be grouped so that each section only takes a few minutes to accomplish. These groups of steps should also refer or correlate to specific test goals delineated in the test plans.

When organizing test procedures, it may be helpful for you to refer back to your HIPO package. If complete, this package can provide the necessary information to functionally group your testing, and can assist you in determining the expected outputs based on particular inputs. Remembering to test for both positive and negative conditions, you may find that organizing your test inputs in the same sequence will help you to cover all the bases. This sequence is: normal values, valid but slightly abnormal values, and invalid values. These groups should correspond to the tolerable limits also specified in your test plan.

Normal values are all those middle of the road values that can reasonably be expected during the operation of the program. For example, the number of overtime hours an employee works should be between .5 and 40 (according to Figure 4-9). Testing for normal values could involve input values of one and ten. Tests for valid but slightly abnormal values could include input values of .5 and 40 (this is also known as testing the limits of a variable). Finally, your variable testing should include values that are outside the tolerable limits. In this case, the values .3 and 82 are outside the valid range for overtime hours.

In addition to Extended Descriptions on HIPOs, you can prepare for logic-path testing—specifically decision-point testing—by referring to your decision tables. These tabular representations of decision paths have only one outcome per unique set of conditions. Thus, your test procedures can be structured to take each unique path through your program logic. As many paths as possible should be tested. However, because of the volumes of testing required to perform testing on every combination of decision criteria throughout your program, it is testing of this sort that usually is left for the end. As such, logic-path testing is rarely completed.

If your program anticipates that a file of data already exists, you may need to create a *test file* of data. This test file should be large enough to provide an adequate combination of test data, but small enough to be processed within short testing periods. If you are testing outputs such as hard-copy reports, your test file should be large enough to more than fill one page. Often programs do not account for extra lines of data on a printed report. Your test data should exercise this "unusual" condition. Similarly, if an exception report is to be tested, be sure to have enough "exception data" to adequately exercise your report coding.

FIGURE 10-2. Tabular Method of Specifying Test Procedures.

Test # _III-1_   Program ID: _Employee Payroll_ Date: _10-15-83_

INPUT	PROCESSING	EXPECTED OUTPUT	ACTUAL OUTPUT
1. overtime hours = 1.0	accepted, ready for new input		
2. overtime hours = 10.0	accepted, ready for new input		
3. overtime hours = .5	accepted, ready for new input		
4. overtime hours = 40	accepted, ready for new input		
5. overtime hours = 82	rejected—error message displayed	"Excessive Overtime Hours"	

Approved by _____

Date _____

The final step in preparing your test procedures is to compose a script of what should take place in the test session. The first item on this script should be an explanation of how to turn on the computer, followed by an explanation of how to start your program. After these two primary steps, the format of your test script depends on your personal preference. You may find the tabular method shown in Figure 10-2 to be most effective, or you may find pictorial representations of the display screens (as shown in Figure 10-3) to be

FIGURE 10-3. Display Screen for Entry of Time Card Information.

```
      *** EMPLOYEE TIME CARD INFORMATION ***

      Social Security No.: _ _ _ _ _ _ _ _ _
      Regular Hours: _ _
      Vacation: _ _
      Sick Leave: _ _
      Overtime: _ _

      (error message)
```

easier to use. In either case, space should be saved on the form for your initials to signify approval or for correction verification.

PERFORMING TESTING

The drudgery ends with this final step. Now you are able to see how your program will respond to the planned inputs. If all goes well, your planned outputs will be the results of the exercising the program code. When you do sit down to test your program, pretend you have never seen the test plans and procedures before. Also pretend you do not know anything about your program code. Follow your plan and its respective steps exactly as it is structured. Also, record the responses of your program exactly as they occur, and in the appropriate table or figure.

If you can, make only minor changes to your program during the test sessions. It is often wise to collect the results of your test and go back to your desk to work on the error resolution. You will be able to think through errors and isolate bugs more easily if you are situated away from the active testing environment. Occasionally, it may be necessary to repeat the test in order to better isolate the problem.

Always repeat prior tests after you have made a correction. It is not necessary to repeat dozens of tests each time you make a change. Instead, consider a strategy whereby some tests are performed with each modification. This will assure that eventually all tests are performed several times. If additional problems are encountered, concentrate on what was changed in order to resolve the original error. That isolated change can often be the clue for what is now wrong. Again, once the problem is resolved, repeat some of the tests until you are satisfied that the program works properly.

Post-Handling

Now that your test session is finished, you can breathe more easily, but your work is not yet finished. Even if you uncovered no bugs, you must still write down what transpired during the testing process. The importance of this documentation cannot be overemphasized. Figure 10-4 suggests an easy way of documenting your test session. There are many advantages to completing a form such as this. First, you will be able to chronologically track your testing pro-

FIGURE 10-4. Post-Test Session Documentation Form.

TEST SESSION REPORT

Tester: _____

Date: _____ Time: _____

Accomplishments: _____
_____
_____
_____

Problems Noted/Resolved: _____
_____
_____
_____
_____

Plan for Next Session: _____
_____
_____
_____

---

grams. Second, you can easily note where a problem seems to be recurring. Although it is unlikely, the problem may be hardware-related. If so, good documentation of the problem symptoms can expedite the repair process. The third advantage is that the form encourages you to consider what you plan to accomplish for the next session. This will help you to maintain testing momentum, a real asset when the going gets rough.

Keep in mind that testing requires planning and preparation. You will be unable to do an adequate job if you approach testing haphazardly. Plan complete tests that will exercise all the little details of your program logic. Prepare your test steps by writing test procedures. Prepare for successful testing by adopting a positive attitude toward this process, and by conveying that attitude toward those who may help you.

While you are testing, don't panic if your program fails. Sit back, take a deep breath, and think. Try not to jump to any conclusions or solutions. It is all too easy to read conditions into the situation that may lead you on to an unproductive tangent. Often it is helpful to repeat the test and force your program to fail a second time, or a third, so that you can get a clear idea of where or how your program is failing.

If you simply cannot resolve the problem, take some time to clear your head. Have a cup of coffee or take a short walk. If you have a friend who has the time to listen, try explaining the problem. You may be surprised how often you will stop in the middle of your own sentence and realize what you have been doing wrong. If that doesn't happen, go on to something else for a while. When you come back to the problem you will approach it with a different outlook and may find your solution quickly.

Once you've made necessary modifications to your code, go back and assure yourself that you have not changed any expected actions of the program. Repeat previous tests that provide a broad rechecking of previous performance. Then retest that portion that failed. Always stick closely to your test plans and procedures. If you discover they are inadequate, write new ones.

A natural inclination, particularly of beginning programmers, is to believe that most problems are caused by hardware failures. The ratio of software to hardware problems is probably on the order of 95:5. The vast majority of program failures are due to software failure, so while hardware does occasionally break down, it is always best to assume that the error is caused by software. In the case of programming, the hardware is innocent until proven guilty.

Always try to repeat the problem before you try to develop a solution. And by all means, look on testing as a fun and challenging activity. There's no sense in your having to struggle through a necessary part of program development. Keep a positive attitude, and remember: your program will be much better once it's been thoroughly tested.

CONCLUSION

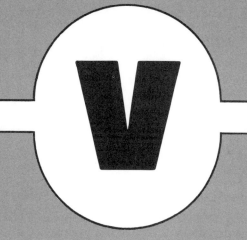

Loose Ends and Last Words

11

You have come a long way toward understanding the design and development of computer programs. By now you are well-equipped to design programs that will be both flexible and efficient. As with most novice program designers, your enthusiasm may prove to be counterproductive. This last chapter is devoted to topics that are independently important, but do not warrant treatment in separate chapters. These topics include a brief discussion of documentation, your attitudes toward program development, and your noncomputer life.

DOCUMENTATION

It is very appropriate that the discussion of documentation be left for the final chapter. This is because almost without fail, documentation is put off until the program is designed, coded, and tested. The two types of documentation referred to here are generic types, detailed or technical, and user-oriented.

You are already familiar with many components of technical documentation. The design tools presented in this book are an excellent, comprehensive collection of technical or detailed design documentation. What you may not realize, however, is the importance of documenting your program code. Programming languages provide a means for you to insert English text among your coding statements. The BASIC language uses the "command" REM, or REMark, for this purpose. Similarly, the COBOL compiler will not interpret the contents of a line in your program beginning with an asterisk. It is important that you learn what feature your programming language uses. More important, though, is that you use this comment feature.

It is not necessary for you to comment on every line of code. However, when you first begin coding, commenting for every line will get you into the habit of providing *in-line documentation.* General in-line documentation practices call for a few sentences of explanation at the beginning of every routine and subroutine analogous to every function and subfunction on the structure diagram. In this routine documentation, you should note what the routine does, under what conditions the routine is called, what variable values are expected, what other subroutines are called, and what the calling routine can expect as output from this routine. These items should be consistently documented even if the item is not pertinent. For example, Figure 11-1 shows a suggested format for documenting in the program listing the specifics of the subroutine DISPERR. Note how although no subroutines are to be called by this subroutine, that item is still included in the description. Such consistency assures the reader that no important information has been overlooked.

In-line documentation should not stop at the subroutine level. It is also important for you to explain why sections of code are there, especially in complex decision logic. For example, it may not be obvious by reading program code that you are checking the input,

FIGURE 11-1. Sample In-Line Documentation Subroutine Description Using BASIC REM Statements.

```
10 REM      SUBROUTINE NAME: DISPERR
20 REM      PURPOSE: This subroutine is responsible for display-
30 REM              ing the desired error message on the
40 REM              terminal. It should only be called when
50 REM              another section of the program has de-
60 REM              tected an error of input that needs atten-
65 REM              tion by the program operator.
70 REM      EXPECTED INPUT: Variable DISPNUM should be
80 REM              set to the numeric value of the message
90 REM              to be displayed. Valid range is 1-9.
100 REM     SUBROUTINES CALLED: None
110 REM     RESULTANT OUTPUT: Variable DISPNUM is
112 REM             cleared to zero after the message has been
113 REM             displayed.
```

Social Security number, against that on the Employee Master File for a match. It is best in cases like this to precede the coding statements for that logic with a comment describing that section of code. Likewise, comments should be included in table or array definitions.

You may question the need for documenting so succinctly the program code that is so much a part of you. While you have probably written fairly detailed descriptions throughout the design process, it has probably changed significantly since you first developed one of the tools. True, you should be keeping that documentation up to date, but time may prohibit you from doing this. Besides, changing a few lines of code here and there may not seem to warrant changing two or three pages of flowcharts or HIPOs. So, you should keep your in-line documentation up-to-date so that anyone (including yourself) will be able to easily read your program listing and understand how you ultimately approached the resolution to the problem definition. Remember that your approach is probably unique. If you were trying to fix or modify someone else's code, you would appreciate that person clarifying program information for you. For example, it would be helpful to know all the ways that a particular general purpose variable could be used in the program. So even if you don't anticipate giving your code to another person, keep in mind that your coding expertise will mature with every new program you write. Do yourself a favor and utilize in-line documentation.

The last type of technical documentation increases in value as more people become involved in the program-design process. This documentation has no formal name, other than perhaps a *project notebook*. In this notebook you should keep informal notes or copies of formal memos delineating why certain design decisions were made. This may seem trivial at first, but it is a good habit to acquire. Too often on larger projects you may find yourself asking, "Why did I decide to do that? Wouldn't it be better if I had done this?" It would be much easier for you to open your notebook and remind yourself why you made a decision rather than have to go through the process a second time. Save yourself frustration and valuable time by jotting down notes so that you have a program-design memory. Don't rely on brainpower—write it down. Besides, notes written at the time of the decision are usually more accurate than what might result when you attempt to redo that design.

Now that your programming task (both current and future) has been simplified, consider how you can make the use of your program simpler. Documentation will certainly help. You can think of user documentation as a training tool, or at least a security blanket. If you are like most people, sitting down at a microcomputer to use a program for the first time can be a frightening and frustrating experience—especially if there is no guide telling you how to use a program. User documentation is the answer, or at least it should provide all of the answers to a variety of questions, ranging from "How do I turn on the computer?" to "How do I stop the program?"

Before you become discouraged and think you have tremendous amounts of original writing to do, think back to your written test plans and procedures. If those were clearly and concisely written, the battle may be nearly won. Pull out those design tools, more commonly referred to as scissors and tape, decide on the format you want to use, and beef up your test plans and procedures so that they are more easily read by humans (a condition known as *user friendly*).

A great deal of experimentation has taken place over the past few years in documenting microcomputer programs. Too often, the user documentation has been written by the programmer who wrote the program. This is not necessarily bad, as long as the writer remembers that those steps obvious to him or her (such as calling up the first menu screen) may not be obvious to others. When you write user documentation, remember that another user may not have the same in-depth knowledge of computers and program design that you have. If you think you will be the only user of the program, consider that your friends or co-workers may also want a copy of your program. Or, remember that it may be six months or a year later when you refer to it again. In either case, time invested in writing user documentation during the development of the program will pay off each time you reach for that documentation in the future.

User documentation is important, but what should it look like? That, of course, depends on your personal biases. Find examples of user documentation and examine them closely. Even better, try to use the program with only the aid of that documentation and see how successful you are. When you write documentation, you will find that the more pictures of what the user will see on the display screen that you include, the faster the user will be able to assimilate the information (imagine having read this book without the aid of pictures and figures). Consistency of format is essential. Whether you include lists, pictures, or paragraph descriptions of what the user is to expect, use that same format throughout.

With user documentation there is a fine line between too little and too much description. What may be necessary to train the novice user may prove to be too cumbersome for an experienced user. The ideal combination is an overview of what the program does, a description of how each function is used, and a reference section for quick problem resolution. The overview should give the reader an understanding of what functions are available. This can usually be accomplished by modifying the problem definition so that it can be easily understood by a noncomputer-oriented user (another example of user friendliness).

The explanation of the functions should be presented as the user will see them. That is, if a menu, such as that shown in Figure 11-2, is the entry point for the various functions, it should be shown so that the user knows what to expect. Then, the functions should be presented in the same order as they appear on the menu screen. The explanation of each function should include all screens that may appear during the use of that function. It is best to walk the user through an example step-by-step, contrasting what is presented by the computer with what is entered by the user. This description is best presented by guiding the reader through an example. As the payroll example was used throughout this book, a single example should be used throughout the user document. In order to speed up writing of these sections, consider using the test plans and procedures you have already written.

The final portion of the user document should be a reference section explaining the various error messages that may appear during the use of your program. The description of each error message should include instructions on how to resolve the error. For ex-

FIGURE 11-2. Sample Payroll System Menu.

```
              *** PAYROLL SYSTEM MENU ***

      WHICH DO YOU WISH TO DO?

              1.  ENTER NEW EMPLOYEE
              2.  LIST EMPLOYEES—YTD AMOUNTS
              3.  LIST EMPLOYEES—CURRENT PERIOD AMOUNTS
              4.  PRODUCE WEEKLY PAYROLL
              5.  TERMINATE EMPLOYEE
              6.  UPDATE EMPLOYEE INFORMATION

      ENTER SELECTION HERE: _____
```

ample, you may need to tell the user to re-key a field (e.g., the Social Security number) and ensure that only numerals appear before transmitting.

In general, user documentation should be thorough enough for the novice user, but brief enough so that it will be easy for the experienced user to reference. Whatever format you select, be consistent throughout your document. If your program is part of a larger system, be sure to follow the standards, or conventions, already established. The document not only should be used to learn the system and resolve problems, but also should be kept current so that it can be used as a training tool for new users.

ATTITUDES

Successful programmers, whether they are hobbyists or professionals, eventually adopt certain attitudes toward their work. These are usually learned through experience. This section discusses a few of these attitudes—a discussion aimed at stimulating your thinking.

If you do not recall reading warnings about mixing your ego with your work, you should go back and look for these words of caution. It is important that you separate your sense of self-worth from the value of your program. Conversely, you must remember not to criticize another programmer for his or her design work. Keep in mind that everyone thinks differently and will develop unique approaches to logic flow. Demeaning remarks serve no purpose except to deflate one's ego and squelch creativity.

Program design and development is a learning activity, no matter how many programs you design. Each effort should be an attempt to better your last effort. Involve others in the process so that you can learn new perspectives and approaches. If someone asks for your assistance, be flattered, but instead of telling that person that your ideas are superior to his or hers, try to guide that person's reasoning so that he or she "discovers" those same ideas. Rather than instructing someone to do something a certain way, ask questions, such as "What would happen if . . ." This approach is less threatening and opens the topic for discussion. Often, you may learn that your approach is not feasible or has already been rejected for good reasons. On occasions when your approach is adopted, keep in mind that the process has been an educational one for everyone involved, including yourself.

This should demonstrate that program design and development is a continuing learning process. Just as you may appreciate the respect of others listening to you, always listen to those people who are assisting you. Even when you think you have the best design, you may learn something by keeping your ears open. Further, if you don't understand something or run into problems, freely admit to this and proceed to learn from someone else.

There are no dumb questions. Every question should be welcomed with an open, nonjudgmental attitude. You were a beginner once, and so is every person involved in learning programming and designing. Once you become more proficient, be willing to share your knowledge with others. One of the best ways to test your knowledge and understanding of a topic is to explain it to another person.

Finally, never assume that you know it all. In this field, at just about the time you feel confident that you have mastered a task, technology leaps ahead. These leaps will eventually affect you in your seemingly isolated microcomputer environment. Think back for a moment about the technological advances of the past five to ten years. Program design and development practices have advanced nearly as rapidly as advances in hardware. Even the tools and techniques presented in this book have, for the most part, been used only during the past ten years.

YOUR OTHER LIFE

Yes, there is life apart from the microcomputer. Many people have become addicted to working with computers over the past few decades. Whereas this addiction used to be confined to the ranks of professionals, now the aura of the computer has invaded homes everywhere. In the 1970s the divorce rate among computer professionals soared. There is no adequate way to determine the negative impact of microcomputers on home life and the family. This is a problem caused by the nature of programming, which is a self-gratifying activity. When working alone on a microcomputer it is easy to become mesmerized. After all, it always does what you tell it to do, it responds immediately to your every command, it is never irrational, and it never resists. Programmers often experience a tremendous sense of power. With the power and positive interaction experienced during computer use, it is very easy to become totally involved, and neglect family and friends.

This *submersion syndrome* can be disastrous to personal relationships. You must remember that you are still a human being who requires interaction with other people. Don't let the computer throw your life completely out of balance. It is all too easy to keep working on a program throughout the night. Be careful to exercise self-discipline, and force yourself to leave your computer work for at least a few hours every day.

You should also be cautious not to start using your newly acquired computer jargon around folks who do not understand it. This is not only threatening, but rude. By using such jargon and making excessive computer puns, you may appear to be an elitist. This can act to your disadvantage, as everyone around you will not share your enthusiasm and may decide that you—and computers—are distasteful and obnoxious. Machines are not capable of reaching out and touching you, giving encouragement or support, or providing needed affection. As a human being, these facets of your life must also be fulfilled.

Finally, if you are considering computers as a profession, there are some things you should know about the programming environment. First, where microcomputers are used in corporations, it is often with application packages that require little or no original design and development. These application packages are systems which are ready to operate once you load them into the computer. Examples include: payroll, inventory control, accounts receivable, and so on.

Second, programming on mainframes is somewhat different from programming on microcomputers. Usually, mainframe programs developed by individual programmers are part of a larger system. This means that you will probably not be allowed to work independently. Professional programmers must interact daily with others in the same field. For people determined to enter a profession in which they believe they will interact with machines instead of other people, this comes as a rude awakening. Furthermore, this human interaction is often more difficult than usual because programmers tend to be quite bright, sometimes less tolerant of others, and show a preference to work with computers instead of human beings.

Third, programming requires a great deal of dedication and patience. You must be willing to sit still for long periods of time, and to work long and odd hours. Programming projects are seldom estimated accurately, resulting in lots of work being required at the last minute in order to meet deadlines. Once the program is being used, the programmer is usually responsible for resolving errors whenever they occur. Unfortunately, this may require the programmer's presence on the scene in the middle of the night!

The last reality of the programming profession to be discussed here concerns maintenance. Most programming time is spent maintaining programs, many of which were developed by someone else. This type of programming can be very challenging, but also very frustrating. The major source of this frustration comes when a large program crashes and you discover that the documentation is either inadequate or outdated. Of course, an experience of this sort will give you an appreciation of the need for thorough, current documentation.

LEARNING MORE

So you are eager to learn more? Where do you turn? Other books, of course, provide excellent sources of information. Computer courses at local schools offer a structured environment for supplementing knowledge. One of the best ways to learn is to become involved in a local user group or computer club. In this type of environment, you will be able to share knowledge with your peers. This human interaction will encourage you to learn more and give you opportunities to apply that knowledge.

Part of the gratification you receive by working with computers should come from sharing ideas with others. To satisfy this need, find folks who share your enthusiasm. Always remember, though, that a computer club is *not* a surrogate family. Get involved, increase your knowledge, gain as much experience as possible, and enjoy!

Appendices

APPENDIX A: COMPARISON OF COMMON PROGRAMMING LANGUAGES

LANGUAGE	STRENGTHS	WEAKNESSES
BASIC (Beginner's All Purpose Instruction Code)	Easy to learn Available on most micro-computers Interpretive	Not sophisticated May be cumbersome Most dialects not structured
C	Structured language Used for writing operating systems	
COBOL (Common Business-Oriented Language)	Business applications Report generation ANSI standard version available	Verbose Requires a lot of main memory
FORTRAN (Formula Translation)	Scientific application Complex mathematical computations ANSI standard version available	Cryptic for beginners
LISP (List Processor)	Symbolic Artificial intelligence applications	Only data structure is binary tree
Logo	Instruction language for beginners Graphics	Limited in sophistication
Pascal	Structured language Recursive applications Data structure definition Fast compile time	Somewhat sophisticated for beginners Slower execution time than FORTRAN
Pilot	Tutorial programs Easy to use Can do graphics and music	Sophisticated applications Difficult to program

APPENDIX B: ADDITIONAL ACTION VERBS

VERB	MEANING
_____	_____
_____	_____
_____	_____
_____	_____
_____	_____
_____	_____
_____	_____
_____	_____
_____	_____
_____	_____

APPENDIX C: ANSI STANDARD SYSTEM AND PROGRAM FLOWCHARTING SYMBOLS

PROGRAM FLOWCHART SYMBOLS

PROCESS
A group of one or more instructions that perform a processing function

INPUT/OUTPUT
Any function involving an input/output device

DECISION
A point in the program where a branch to alternate paths is possible

PREPARATION
A group of one or more instructions that sets the stage for subsequent processing

PREDEFINED PROCESS
A group of operations not detailed in this flowchart (often, a library subroutine)

TERMINAL
Beginning, end, or point of interruption in a program

CONNECTOR
Entry from, or exit to, another part of the flowchart

ADDITIONAL SYMBOLS FOR SYSTEM AND PROGRAM FLOWCHARTING

FLOWLINE
Direction of processing or data flow

ANNOTATION
Descriptive comments or explanatory ntoes provided for clarification

SYSTEM FLOWCHART SYMBOLS

PROCESS
A major processing function, usually, one computer program

PUNCHED CARD
All varieties of punched cards

DOCUMENT
Paper documents and reports of all kinds

MAGNETIC TAPE

CORE STORAGE

DISPLAY
Information displayed by plotters or visual-display units

COLLATE
Forming one file from two or more similarly sequenced files

EXTRACT
Forming two or more files from one file

MANUAL OPERATION
A manual offline operation not requiring mechanical aid

MANUAL INPUT
Data supplied to or by a computer by means of an online device

INPUT/OUTPUT
Any type of medium or data

PUNCHED TAPE
Paper or plastic tape, chad or chadless

OFFLINE STORAGE

ONLINE STORAGE

MAGNETIC DISK

MAGNETIC DRUM

SORT
Arranging data items by means of sorting or collating equipment

MERGE
Combining two or more similarly sequenced files into one file in the same order (special case of collate)

AUXILIARY OPERATION
A machine operation supplementing the main processing function

COMMUNICATION LINK
Automatic transmission of data from one location to another

Marilyn Bohl, *A Guide for Programmers,* © 1978, p. 72. Reprinted by permission of Prentice-hall, Inc., Englewood Cliffs, N.J.

Glossary

Abort. Abnormal termination; usually the result of processing "getting lost." For example, if an inappropriate machine instruction causes the computer to attempt to interpret data as machine instructions, it may eventually find data which does not comprise an understandable instruction. The computer will be forced to stop.

Accumulator. A register, or storage location, in which the result of an arithmetic or logic operation is formed.

Address Space. The complete range of addresses available to a programmer. In microcomputers, the maximum is usually limited by the number of bits designated for RAM location within an instruction.

Algorithm. A set of well-defined rules or processes in the form of a computer program for the solution of a problem in a finite number of steps.

Alpha. Refers to alphabetic characters, A through Z.

Alphanumeric. Refers to letters and numerals, A through Z and zero through nine.

American Standard Code for Information Processing. See ASCII.

Analysis. The methodical investigation of a situation, usually involving identification of smaller related units for further detailed study.

ANSI. American National Standards Institute.

Applications. Computer programs written for or by a user that perform certain functions by telling the computer how to do a specific job.

Application system. A group of programs and associated documentation pertaining to a specific problem. For example, a payroll system providing paycheck production, W-2 generation, and employee information entry and update.

Architecture. The physical design of the computer, especially considering how instructions in memory are interpreted by the processor.

Array. A named, ordered collection of data elements. Each entry in the array has the same data elements, arranged in the same order.

ASCII. The standard code used for information interchange among data-processing systems. The code character set consists of 96 displayed characters and 32 non-displayed control characters using eight bits, including parity check.

Auxiliary Storage. Area external to the computer where programs and data may be saved.

Backup. The duplication of files on separate volumes so that recovery of programs and data can be speedy should failure occur.

BASIC (Beginner's All-purpose Instruction Code). A common, high-level computer programming language developed by Dartmouth College. There are over 100 dialects of this language.

Bidirectional. Refers to printers that print left-to-right and right-to-left, alternating lines of print. Scheme used to hasten hard copy printed by taking advantage of the time normally wasted in returning the printer device to the left column.

Binary. A numbering system using only the symbols 0 and 1. Since computers store information by positive and negative charges—or on and off—binary lends itself well to numeric representation of these two states.

Binary Decision. A decision point in program logic having only two possible answers: yes or no.

Bit (binary digit). The basic unit of information with which a computer works; either 0 or 1. A group of bits are used to represent a character in the computer.

Black Box. Refers to process or function that later is described in greater detail. In flowcharting, used to illustrate where function should be performed rather than showing how it will be accomplished.

Boards. Short for printed circuit boards. Thin, insulated material on which electrically conducting material is patterned, and electrical components are attached to those patterns.

Boot. Perform an initial load of an operating system so the computer can accept input from external sources.

Bootstrap. See Boot.

Bottom-up Testing. Technique of integration testing where processor modules are tested independently, integrated into functional units and tested, and so on until the entire program or system finally emerges.

bpi. Bits or bytes per inch.

bps. Bits per second.

Branch. An instruction that causes departure from the sequence of instruction being followed. Often the result of a conditional comparison.

Buffer. An area of main storage that is temporarily reserved for use in performing the input-output operation, into which data are read or from which data are written.

Bug. A program error causing the input, processing, or output to be improperly performed.

Byte. Eight adjacent bits. Each unique combination either represents a character, an instruction, or an address in memory.

Calculations. Mathematical processes performed on data.

Call. Activate processing of a module or subroutine through program coding references. Control is returned to the calling module at the point of departure.

Case Logic. A string of binary decisions, each testing for a value of the same variable.

Cassette Tape. Auxiliary storage medium; magnetic tape similar to that used to record music or voice.

Cathode Ray Tube. See CRT.

Character. An individual letter, numeral, or special symbol, represented by a unique byte value.

Character Set. All the characters recognized by a computer system. Each is given a unique numeric representation. The number of bits required for this representation typically defines the size of the byte.

Coding. Actual writing of computer program statements in a particular computer language.

Common Processor. Symbol in structure diagram used the first time a commonly used processor is cited in the structure diagram.

Compilation. Preparation of a machine language program from a high-level, symbolic language by converting each instruction into a series of machine-language instructions.

Compiler. A program that converts high-level symbolic language statements into multiple machine-language instructions.

Computer. An electronic machine used for performing a variety of functions that are limited by only the creativity of its programmers.

Conditional Transfer. See Branch.

Configuration. A collection of peripheral devices, along with a computer, which comprise a computer system.

Constants. Variables having the same value, regardless of processing conditions.

Continuous Form. Paper that is used on printers, which has small holes on the outer edges for automatic feeding of the paper. Can be blank sheets or preprinted forms such as invoices or checks.

Control. A program or module that is currently being executed by the computer.

Convention. A programming style rule, providing consistency among different programs.

Conversational Mode. Communication between a terminal user and a computer in which the input from the terminal elicits a timely response from the computer, and vice versa.

Conversion. The process of changing from one method of data processing to another, or from one computer system to another.

Counter. A location in the computer that accumulates the number of occurrences of an event.

cpi. Characters per inch.

Crash. Cessation of operation resulting from hardware or software failures.

CRT. A visual display device similar to a television screen on which visual images are presented for the user to understand. May be either monochromatic or colored.

Cylinder. All tracks on a magnetic disk that can be accessed by the read/write heads with one movement or positioning of the access mechanism.

DA. See Direct Access.

Data (plural of datum). Combinations of numbers, letters, and symbols that are to be processed by a computer program. The term datum is seldom used, but if it were, it would refer to a byte.

Data Base. Collection of interrelated data items processable by more than one application program.

Data Base Management System. Software that establishes and employs rules about file organization and processing. Also establishes relationships between files and records in each file. Some systems employ special instructions that may be used in application programs to access data.

Data Element. Discrete pieces of information, usually consisting of a number of bytes, which is part of a data record or file. (Also called a field.)

Data File. See File.

Data Integrity. See Integrity.

Data Item. The smallest unit of named data such as a variable. It may consist of any number of bits or bytes.

Data Rate. The rate at which a channel carries data, measured in bits per second.

Data Storage. The preservation of data on various external media that can later be accessed by the computer.

Debugging. The act of detecting, isolating, and resolving an error in a program.

Decimal. Numbering system based upon the first ten numerals.

Decimal Digit. One of the characters zero through nine.

Dedicated. Usually referring to a program or peripheral device that functions within the realm of a particular mainframe.

Default. The value or action to be assumed appropriate unless otherwise specified or instructed.

Delivery. Final step in program-development cycle where program or system is given to the users for execution against actual data.

Density. The number of information units per physical measurement (for example, 6250 bpi).

Desk Checking. A debugging technique that involves reading through design work or program code at one's desk, alone.

Device. A peripheral component of a computer system.

Diagnostic. Software programs that are used to determine the location of a computer or peripheral malfunction. Also pertains to error messages generated at program compilation or assembly.

Dialect. A particular version of a programming language, with its unique rules and words. Usually a minor modification of some base language like BASIC or Pascal, but because of vast differences in modifications it may be significantly different from other dialects of same language.

Digit. A character representing a quantity or numeral. For binary, zero through one; decimal, zero through nine; hexadecimal, zero through F.

Direct Access. File organization that uses portions of records to calculate the exact location of the particular record.

Disk. Peripheral storage media containing magnetic disks on which data are stored. Some are fixed, or permanently attached to the device, while others are removable "packs."

Diskette. A small, flexible rotating platter on which data or programs are stored magnetically. Storage capacity depends on size, density, and number of sides used for storage.

Display. A visual presentation of data in the form of lights illuminated on a computer or text presented on a video display unit.

Display Unit. The physical device upon which information is displayed for the user to see. Often in the form of a CRT, and may include a keyboard.

Documentation. Usually refers to design tools and manuals associated with programs, but may also include remarks or comments included within a program.

Dot Matrix. A method of printing output characters on hard copy using positional combinations of dots.

Double-density. Refers to storage capacity of diskettes with twice the standard number of tracks per side.

Double-sided. Both sides of the diskette are used for reading and writing information. As such, affords twice the storage capacity of single-sided diskettes.

Downtime. A period of time in which a computer is not operating correctly or is malfunctioning due to hardware or software failure.

Drive. The physical components necessary for reading and writing information to and from a diskette or disk.

Driver. Software that usually is in ROM, which allows the computer to communicate with a particular peripheral device.

Dummy Module. Skeleton of module with entry and exit, but no actual processing. Particularly useful in top-down testing when subordinate subfunctions and processors are not ready for integration.

Else Clause. The action that is to be performed if the decision-condition statement is not true.

Endurance Testing. Ensuring through trial operation that the program or system will continue to perform reliably over an extensive, continuous period of operation.

Enhancement. See Enhancing.

Enhancing. Improving on an original program either by modifying existing code or adding new code to an existing program.

Error Detection. Techniques that assist in identification, isolating, and correction of program bugs. Requires desire to locate errors to be effective.

Escape. Special action of the computer-user requesting that control be returned to the main controller or to the operating system.

Evolutionary Approach. Technique of integration testing where modules are added to the core as they are coded. Testing is performed on progressively larger core.

Exception. Anything that is out of the ordinary. For example, invalid items or values out of acceptable limits.

Execute. See Run.

Field. See Data Element.

File. A collection of data records, each containing similar sets of information, and saved on an auxiliary-storage device.

File Directory. A list of files on a particular auxiliary-storage medium indicating to the operating system the physical location of all files contained therein.

Flag. A variable having a specific meaning, depending upon its value to decision processing in another part of the program or module.

Floppy Diskette. See Diskette.

Flowchart. A pictorial representation of the logic flow within a system, program, or module.

Flowchart Symbol. The shapes that represent specific items and, when combined with logic flow, comprise a system, program, or module flowchart.

Formatting Characters. Special characters that are used to make program output more legible to humans. For example, $,.

Function. A program unit providing a unique capability.

Hard Coded. Specific values included in program statements. In order to change them, a change in the source code, and possibly recompiling, must be made.

Hard Copy. Any output that can be taken away from the computer in a form visually readable by humans.

Hardware. The physical equipment, including mechanical, electrical, or magnetic devices. May refer to the computer, its peripheral devices, or both.

Head. A small electromagnet capable of reading, writing, or erasing data on auxiliary-storage media.

Hexadecimal. Pertaining to a number system with a base of 16. Valid digits range from zero through F, where F represents the highest unit's value (15). Also referred to as "hex."

High-level Language. Computer programming languages such as BASIC, COBOL, Logo, and Pascal which allow the programmer to express operations in a form that is closer to normal human language.

HIPO. Hierarchy plus Input Process Output. A design tool consisting of a visual table of contents, input-process-output diagrams and extended descriptions.

Increment. To add a value (usually one) to the current value of a variable or counter.

Idiot Check. A condition test included in the code for all those impossible conditions. Helps to protect the program from aborting.

Idle Time. That part of available time during which the hardware is not being used.

If-then-else. See Binary Decision.

Indexed Sequential. Sequential data-file organization with a preface table indicating the approximate location of the desired record (identified by the record's key).

Infinite Loop. The programmer's nightmare, where the same set of instructions is performed repeatedly with no condition that will allow an exit branch.

Information. Data that has been organized and presented in a meaningful way.

Initialize. Set the value of a variable when the program is first executed. May be done through compilation.

In-line Documentation. Documenting program code using comment or remark statements within source statements.

Input. Data external to the program that are to be processed.

I/O (Input/Output). The passing of data between peripheral equipment and the computer, and vice versa.

I/O Channel. A portion of computer equipment over which input and output are transmitted.

Installation. A particular computing system, including the equipment and the people who manage, operate it, apply it to problems, service it, and use the results it produces.

Integration Testing. Collecting functional units and testing them as a whole unit to ensure they perform properly together.

Integrity. Preservation of data or programs for their intended use.

Interpretation. Translation of high-level language statements to machine-level instructions as each high-level statement is executed (as opposed to compilation).

Interactive. Pertaining to an application in which each entry elicits a response, as in an airline reservation system.

Interrupt. A temporary break in the normal processing of a computer program so that the processing can be resumed from the point of interruption at a later time. Usually the result of input from an external source.

ISAM. Indexed Sequential Access Method. See Indexed Sequential.

Job. Refers to a unit of work for the computing system, from the standpoint of accounting and/or operating system control.

Joy Stick. A peripheral device used to control the movement of programmed indicators, such as a rocket in a space game.

K. Two raised to the tenth power ($2^{10} = 1024$), roughly representing one thousand or one kilo.

Key. The act of entering information into a program via a keyboard. Also, portions of record combined to provide a unique identifier for each record. In sorting, the data elements used to order the file.

Keyboard. The physical device similar to a typewriter through which the operator can communicate information to the program.

Key Words. Words used in pseudocode or programming languages bearing a specific meaning to the reader or the compiler/interpreter, respectively.

KISS. Common acronym meaning, Keep It Simple Stupid.

Kluge. A sloppy, quick-fix solution to a programming problem. Often used to fix a program bug.

Label. One or more characters used to identify a program, a module, a statement, or a data item.

Language. A set of words and rules that can ultimately be translated to a form understood by a computer.

Large-scale Computer. The grand daddy end of the hardware spectrum. For example, IBM 33xx, Burroughs 6700, and Univac 1100/xx mainframes.

Laser Printer. A type of non-impact printer that combines laser beams and electrophotographic technology to form images on paper.

Letter-Quality. Type of printing produced by striking image of character against ribbon and paper for hard-copy output. Appears as regular typing, and is usually more easily read than dot-matrix print.

Life-cycle. The course of a program or system from the inception of the original idea through development, implementation, and maintenance, until it is either replaced or no longer useful.

Light Pen. A pen-shaped object with a photoelectric cell at its end used to draw on a special CRT.

Line Printer. A computer peripheral device that prints an entire line of characters as a unit at the same time.

Listing. A printout, usually of program source or object code, prepared by the computer.

Logic. See Program Logic.

Logical Units. Functional entities on a structure diagram that can be isolated and programmed as independent functions.

Loop. In programming, a sequence of computer instructions that repeats itself until a predetermined condition is satisfied.

Machine Language. The final language all digital computers must use, in binary. Combinations of zeroes and ones will not always mean the same instruction to all computers.

Magnetic Tape. Flexible plastic tape with a magnetic surface on which data can be stored by selective polarization of portions of the surface.

Main Control. Upper-most box of a structure chart representing the function that has ultimate control over functions performed by a program or system.

Manual Input. Data entered manually by the operator or programmer to modify, continue, or resume processing of a computer system.

Master File. Portion of auxiliary storage containing related data elements that remain reasonably constant over time. Usually refers to file of primary importance within a system.

Master Record. Those data elements related to a specific person or thing that are stored in the master file.

Medium-scale Computers. Slower and physically smaller than large-scale computers like IBM 433x, Univac 90/xx computers.

Memory. Physical devices, both in the computer and peripherals, that hold data and programs in binary format.

Memory Dump. A listing of the contents of a storage device or selected parts of it. Also referred to as dump.

Merge. The operation of combining two or more files of data into one in a predetermined sequence.

Message. A sequence of characters used to convey information or data, usually to the program user.

Microcomputer. The smallest computers that can be programmed for particular uses. Usually only one terminal can be active at a time.

Microfiche. A rectangular transparency (approximately 4" x 6") containing multiple columns of greatly reduced computer printer output images; also may include preprinted forms or images.

Minicomputer. A small, general-purpose computer typically used for dedicated applications. For example, a VAX 11/780 used for educational purposes.

Model. Special simulation programs that allow easy modification of data and recalculation of figures. Most commonly used in financial projections.

Module. A programming unit that is unique in its functionality.

Motherboard. The main board, or chassis, of a microcomputer into which other boards providing other functions are attached.

MTU. See Magnetic Tape Unit.

Negative Testing. Ensuring that unexpected data does not cause program to abnormally terminate.

Nesting. Designing loops within loops. The superior loop is only cycled after the subordinate loop is completed cycling. Or, the subordinate loop is cycled fully with each single iteration of the superior loop.

Nibble. Four adjacent bits; half of a byte.

Numeric. Refers to numerals zero through nine.

On-line. In direct communication with the computer.

Operating System. A program that controls the execution of other computer programs, and which may provide scheduling, debugging, I/O control, accounting, compilation, storage assignment, data management, and related services.

Output. The result of program processing. May be visible to the operator or stored data.

Overconfident Approach. Technique of integration testing where all modules are thrown into one system for testing as a whole. This approach seldom saves any time.

Overflow. The condition where a needed auxiliary storage track has been filled to capacity.

Overflow Tracks. Area within file reserved for use only when track is filled with data. Usually utilized when adding many new records to a file.

Parallel Test. Usually only performed when a new system is being installed, or if a new computer is being used. Requires performing processing in both the old and new way, using the same input data set, and ensuring the results are the same.

Pascal. A powerful, general-purpose, high-level language first developed by Niklaus Wirth.

Password. A unique word or string of characters that must be supplied to be able to access certain data or execute certain programs.

Peripheral Equipment. See Peripherals.

Peripherals. Devices external to, but attached to, the computer which provide a variety of input, output, or related tasks.

Positive Testing. Ensuring expected data is processed properly.

Pre-defined Function. Structure-diagram symbol referring to processor or function on another structure chart. Usually refers to complete structure chart defined elsewhere.

Pre-defined Processor. Symbol in structure diagram used to reference a previously identified common processor.

Prime Tracks. Tracks that are initially used for storing data on a disk file.

Printed Circuit Board. See Boards.

Printer. A peripheral output device that produces hard-copy printed output.

Printout. Printed output from a program.

Process. The manipulation of data by a program.

Processing. The act of the computer executing a program.

Processor. Physical component of a microcomputer by which programs are executed. Also, lowest-level box of structure diagram function or subfunction.

Program. A set of instructions arranged in a specific order to allow a computer to perform certain functions.

GLOSSARY

Programmer. An individual involved in designing, coding, and testing computer programs.

Programming. The preparation of a set of instructions for the computer to use in the solution of a problem.

Program Library. A collection of programs and routines on an auxiliary storage medium.

Program Logic. The program-coding statements arranged in a specific order to perform the input, processing, and output required of a particular problem solution.

Pseudocode. Program-design tool bridging the gap between sentences and program code. More closely resembling a high-level language, but without concern for syntactical rules of a specific language.

RAM. Portion of memory contained in a computer where every program to be executed must reside.

Random Access Memory. See RAM.

Read Head. A head device only capable of reading data.

Read Only Memory. See ROM.

Real-time. The processing of transactions as they occur rather than collecting them. May include immediate modification of data on master files.

Record. Collection of data elements relative to each member of a file.

Redundancy. Repetition of information among various files.

Reliability. Refers to program performing same functions in same manner indefinitely.

Response Time. The amount of time elapsed between generation of an inquiry at a terminal and receipt of response at same terminal.

Restore. Replacing of data or program files from backup auxiliary storage after hardware or software mishap causes loss of original file.

ROM. Portion of memory within the computer that contains computer instructions and cannot be changed by a program.

Routine. See Function.

Run. To cause the program to perform the instructions of a program.

SAM (Sequential Access Method). See Sequential.

Sector. One portion of a disk track.

Security. Refers to making sure the computerized data and program files can't be accessed, obtained, or modified by unauthorized individuals.

Sequential. One step at a time, usually in ascending order. For files, the simplest file organization.

Signature. Pertains to a unique character typically printed in "position one" of a display line, which indicates the control program that will process the next input string.

Simulation. Complex hardware and computer programs that imitate real-life situations.

Single-density. Refers to the standard capacity in data bytes that can be stored on one side of a diskette.

Single-sided. Only one side of the diskette is used for reading and writing information.

Software. Computer programs that make the hardware run.

GLOSSARY

Sort (or sorting). The arrangement of data in numeric, alphabetic, or alphanumeric order according to a specified order.

Source Program. A computer program written in symbolic language that will be converted into a machine-language object program using a compiler or interpreter.

Special Characters. Refers to all characters that are not alpha or numeric, such as $, (,), #, and -.

Storage Capacity. The amount of data that can be contained in a storage device or main memory. Expressed in K bytes or K words.

Storing. Saving data for future reference or use by a program.

Stress Testing. Ensuring through trial operation that the program or system will continue to perform reliably in spite of data inaccuracies and extraordinary data volumes.

Structure Diagram. Design tool defining problem solution in terms of a hierarchial, control-subordinate organization. Helps designer to define the solution in smaller, more manageable units known as functions or modules.

Subfunction. Functional unit of a structure diagram under control of a function other than the main control.

Subroutine. Program unit that performs a specific task. May perform this under the control of various subfunctions within a structure diagram.

Subscript. The item-location identifier for an array entry. In two-dimensional arrays, indicates row and column location within a particular array.

Synthesizer. An output device that produces audible noise resembling voices, musical instruments, and so on.

System. The hardware and software, which together provide computerized functions.

Terminal. A device equipped with a keyboard and some type of display unit (CRT, printer) connected to a computer for the input and/or output of data.

Testing. Exercise of computer programs with intent of finding errors.

Test Plans. General description of what testing will involve, including specification of tolerable limits.

Test Procedures. Detailed description of testing steps, including absolute test inputs and expected results.

Top-down Testing. Technique of integration testing where control modules are tested first, next level is added and tested, and so forth.

Track. A horizontal row running along the length of a magnetic tape, or one of a series of concentric circles on the surface of a disk on which information is written and from which information is retrieved.

Transaction Record. A collection of related data initiating an input activity. May be the result of a series of interactive input responses.

Tree Diagram. Hierarchical structure with one top point and multiple paths below each decision point. More closely resembles roots of tree, rather than branches.

Tweeking. See Enhancing.

Up-time. The time during which a piece of equipment is either operating or available for operation.

User. Anyone who requires the services of a computing system, and who actively accesses the functions provided by programs.

User Friendly. Anything visible to program- or system-users that is presented in a nonthreatening, supportive fashion in an effort to be encouraging and informative but not insulting.

Ultility Program. Specialized program performing a frequently required everyday task.

Variable. A data unit that can assume any of a given set of values.

Video Display Unit. See Display Unit.

VTOC. Visual Table of Contents portion of HIPO package.

Volume. A recording media unit such as a single reel of tape or a single diskette.

Walkthroughs. A technique for having design work reviewed by peers.

Winchester Disk. A particular design of hard disk where the platters are fixed to the unit in a sealed compartment.

Word Processor. Computer program (and sometimes computer hardware) specifically designed for text entry and manipulation.

Write Head. A magnetic device that is only capable of recording on the auxiliary storage medium.

Write. To record data on a storage device, print a record on hard copy, or display data on a terminal.

Bibliography

Albrecht, Karl, *Successful Management by Objectives, An Action Manual.* Englewood Cliffs, New Jersey: Prentice-Hall, Inc., 1978.

Aron, J.D., *The Program Development Process: Part 1, The Individual Programmer.* Reading, Massachusetts: Addison-Wesley Publishing Co. Inc., 1974.

Artwick, Bruce A., *Microcomputer Interfacing.* Englewood Cliffs, New Jersey: Prentice-Hall, Inc., 1980.

Atwood, Jerry W., *The Systems Analyst, How to Design Computer-based Systems.* Rochelle Park, New Jersey: Hayden Book Co., Inc., 1977.

Bohl, Marilyn, *A Guide for Programmers.* Englewood Cliffs, New Jersey: Prentice-Hall, Inc., 1978.

Bohm, C. and G. Jacopini, "Flow Diagrams, Turing Machines, and Languages with Only Two Formulation Rules," *Communications of the ACM,* May 1966, pp. 366-371.

Bohon, Thomas G., "Decision Tables: How to Plan Your Program," in *Programming Techniques: Program Design* (Vol. 1), ed. Blaise W. Liffick. Peterborough, New Hampshire: BYTE Publications, Inc., 1978.

Brooks, Frederick P., Jr., *The Mythical Man-Month.* Reading, Massachusetts: Addison-Wesley Publishing Co. Inc., 1979.

Chapin, Ned, *Computers, A Systems Approach.* New York: Van Nostrand Reinhold Company, 1971.

Covvey, H. Dominic and Neil Harding McAlister, *Computer Consciousness: Surviving the Automated 80s.* Reading, Massachusetts: Addison-Wesley Publishing Co. Inc., 1980.

DeRossi, Claude, J., *Making BASIC Work for You.* Reston, Virginia: Reston Publishing Company, Inc., 1979.

BIBLIOGRAPHY

Dyck, V.A. and others, *Introduction to Computing, Structured Problem Solving Using WATIF-S*. Reston, Virginia: Reston Publishing Company, Inc., 1979.

Feingold, Carl, *Introduction to Data Processing*. Dubuque, Iowa: William C. Brown Co., Publishers, 1976.

Gane, Chris and Trish Sarson, *Structured Systems Analysis: Tools and Techniques*. New York: Improved System Technologies, Inc., 1977.

Gildersleeve, Thomas R., *Successful Data Processing Systems Analysis*. Englewood Cliffs, New Jersey: Prentice-Hall, Inc., 1978.

Hardy, I. Trotter, *Software Tools: A Building Block Approach*. Washington: U. S. Department of Commerce, National Bureau of Standards.

Hearn, Albert D., "Some Words About Program Structure," in *Programming Techniques: Program Design* (Vol. 1), ed. Blaise W. Liffick. Peterborough, New Hampshire: BYTE Publications, Inc., 1978.

Hearn, Albert D., "Top-Down Modular Programming," in *Programming Techniques: Program Design* (Vol. 1), ed. Blaise W. Liffick. Peterborough, New Hampshire: BYTE Publications, Inc., 1978.

Heiserman, David L., *Programming in BASIC for Personal Computers*. Englewood Cliffs, New Jersey: Prentice-Hall, Inc., 1981.

Kapur, Gopal K., *IBM 360 Assembler Language Programming*. New York: John Wiley & Sons, Inc., 1970.

Mager, Robert F., *Goal Analysis*. Belmont, California: Fearon Publishers, 1972.

Mandell, Steven L., *Computers and Data Processing Comcepts and Applications with BASIC*. St. Paul, Minnesota: West Publishing Co., 1979.

"Matrix Printing," *Digital Design*, (March 1979), pp. 50-52.

Katzan, Harry, Jr., *Introduction to Computers and Data Processing*. New York: D. Van Nostrand Company, 1979.

Myers, Glenford J., *The Art of Software Testing*. New York: John Wiley and Sons, Inc., 1979.

Myers, Glenford J., *Software Reliability Principles and Practices*. New York: John Wiley and Sons, Inc., 1976.

Noll, Paul, *Structured Programming for the COBOL Programmer*. Fresno, California: Mike Murach and Associates, Inc., 1977.

Noll, Paul, *The Structured Programming Cookbook*. Fresno, California: Mike Murach and Associates, Inc., 1978.

Page-Jones, Meiler, *The Practical Guide to Structured Systems Design*. New York: Yourdan Press, 1980.

Shneiderman, Ben, *Software Psychology, Human Factors in Computer and Information Systems*. Cambridge, Massachusetts: Winthrop Publishers, Inc., 1980.

Standish, Thomas A., *Data Structure Techniques*. Reading, Massachusetts: Addison-Wesley Publishing Co. Inc., 1980.

Swanson, Robert W., *An Introduction to Business Data Processing and Computer Programming*. Encino, California: Dickenson Publishing Company, Inc., 1967.

Weinberg, Gerald M., *The Psychology of Computer Programming*. New York: Van Nostrand Reinhold Company, 1971.

Wimmert, Robert J., *Computer Programming Techniques.* New York: Holt Reinhart and Winston, 1968.

Wooldridge, Susan, *Systems and Programming Standards.* New York: Petrocelli/Charter, 1977.

Yourdon, Edward, *Managing the Structured Techniques.* Englewood Cliffs, New Jersey: Prentice-Hall, Inc., 1979.

Yourdon, Edward, *Structured Walkthroughs.* Englewood Cliffs, New Jersey, Prentice-Hall, Inc., 1979.

Yourdon, Edward, *Structured Design: Fundamentals of a Discipline of a Computer Program and System Design.* Englewood Cliffs, New Jersey: Prentice-Hall, Inc., 1979.

Yourdon, Edward, *Techniques of Program Structure and Design.* Englewood Cliffs, New Jersey: Prentice-Hall, Inc., 1975.

Index

A
Arrays. *See* Tables
Attitudes, personal, 205-6

B
Backup files, 165
Bit, defines, 5
Boards, 8-9
Bug, defined, 7
Bug indicator, DISPERR function, subroutine, 128
Byte, defined, 5

C
Chips, in computers, discussion, 8-9
Clarity, questions to ask self, 33, 36
Clubs, computer, and user groups, 208
Compilers, 19
Computer languages:
  COBOL, 19
  and compilers, 19
  FORTRAN, 20
  interpretation, 19
Configurations, 15, 16
Constants, defined, 150
Continuation pages, 62-64
  example, 63, 64
Counter variables, defined, 149
CRTs, 9, 10

D
Data, defined, 149
Data, types of:
  elements, 154
  file, 153, 154
  kluges, 156-57
  layout, of master file, 156
  and record description, 154
  records, 154
Data bases, 165-66
Data item attributes, 152-53
  data element, 153
  example, 153
  and number of bytes, 153
Datum, defined, 149
Decision tables, contents and construction of, 99-103, 110-11
  and *vs.* or, 101
  complete table for, 103
  condition combination entries, 101
  defaults, 102
  making decisions, 102
  possible action entries, 100
  skeleton, 100
  steps, 99, 100, 101, 102
Decision tables, enhancing of, 106-10
  discussion, 106-7
  else condition combination, use, 107
  implied ands, 109
  payroll problem, example, 109-10
  unique combinations, 107-8
Decision tables, flowcharting for, 126, 128
Direct access method, 162-64
  characteristics, 163
  diagram, 163
  discussion, 162-63
Disks, 10-11
  storage capacities of, 11
Documentation, 200-5
  error messages, 204-5
  in-line, 201-2
  and menus, 204
  project notebook, 202
  for user, 203-4

E
Error detection:
  clerical, 171

design reviews, 175-77
  formal, log of, 176
  and perspectives, 177
  retrospecing, 177
desk checking, 174-75
  games to play, 174
  perspectives, 174
  walkthroughs, 175
discussion, 170, 171
ego, problems with about, 171-72
logical, 171
methods for, table, 173
perception, problems of, 172
in program life cycle, 170
questions to ask, 173
strengths vs. weaknesses of various methods for, 174
summary, 181
table, 182
tweeks, nature of, 177
walkthroughs, 177-81
  brevity in, 178-79
  compiler errors, 180
  errors, checking for, 180
  frequency, 179
  nature, 177-78
  time for, 179
  use of results, 179
Error messages. *See* Documentation
Extended descriptions. *See* HIPOs

F

Files:
  segmentation, 165
  sizes of, 164-65
  types, 157-58
Flags, defined, 150
Floppies, 11, 12
Flowcharts:
  basic constructs, 120-24
    binary decision, 120, 121
    hard coding, 122
    initializing, 122
    loops, 120, 121
    processing, 120, 121
  decision points, 118
  detail, degrees of, 116, 118-20
  discussion, 113-14
  DOUNTIL, 124
  DOWHILE, 124
  loop limitation methods, 123
  reentry, decision points for, 118
  shower, morning:
    additional detail in chart, 117
    example, 115
  summary, 133-34

symbology, ANSI, 114, 116, 212
system vs. program, compared, 119

G

Goal Analysis, 27

H

Hardware, defined, 6
HIPO (Hierarchy Plus Input Output) package:
  extended descriptions, 83-85, 87, 89
  Input Process Output charts, 69, 77-81, 85-93
    development of, 77-81
    discussion, 77, 85-88
    examples, 78, 80, 81, 85-91
    loops, 82, 83
    for processors, 81-83, 92-93
    temporary files, 83
    summary, 92
  printing order, 70, 72
  structural diagram modification, 70-72
    example, 71
  Visual Table of Contents (VTOC), 69, 72-75
    descriptive section, 76
    logical unit numbering, 73
    steps, 72-73
    structural diagram numbering, 74
Hiring, decision exercise:
  criteria, 103
  table, completed, 104

I

Indexed sequential access method, 160-62
  advantages, 161, 162
  example, 161
  overflow, 161, 162
  characteristics, 162
  tracks in, 160, 161
Information flow, questions and implications, table, 34-35
Input, defined, 6-7
Input Process Output charts, and flowcharts, 128-32. *See also* HIPOs
  discussion, 131, 132
  flowchart symbols, 131, 132
  hiring, example, 129
  payroll problem, validation, 130
Integrity of data, 165

J

Jogging, decision table for, 105-6
Joysticks, 17

L

Languages, common programming, comparison of, 210

M

Mager, Robert, 27
Memory, types, 7-8
Menus, 204

N

Nibble, defined, 5

O

Output, defined, 7

P

Payroll example, for structural diagram:
  discrepancies, 58
  editing of data, 57
  master records, 57
  outputs, production of, 59
  partial development of, 58
  paycheck calculations, 59
  program modules, 56-57
  sequence in, 56
  structural diagram, 60
  transaction records, 57
  tree diagram, 56
Personal life, 206-8
  and programming, points to remember, 207-8
  submersion syndrome, 207
Predefined function symbol, 62
Predefined processor symbol, 61, 62
Printers:
  dot matrix, 13
  letter quality, 13, 14
  samples, 14
  thimbles for, 15
Problem definition:
  ambiguity, reduction of, 25-27
  clarity in, 26, 33, 36
  complete:
    characters per employee, minumum number, 37-38
    final problem definition, 38-39
    procedures requirement, 38
    questions to ask, 36
    storage, amount needed, 37
  discussion, 24-25
  documents for payroll system, identification of, 28
  enhancements, 32
  exceptions, 30
  expansion of, 29, 30, 32
  files, 32-33
  fuzzy, nature of, 27
  information flow, current pattern, 27-38
  internal requirements, 33
  nature, 25
  normal, defined, 30
  outputs, identification of, 31
Problem definitions, summary of:
  alternative outcomes, 39
  data volume, 40
  developmental phase, 40-41
  fuzzy, 39
  length of, 39
  questions to ask, 40
Programs, for computers:
  airplane analogy, 17
  applications, 17
  models, 18
  operating systems, 18
  simulations, 18
  word processors, 18
Programs, defined, 6
Programs, developmental cycle for:
  coding, 21
  documentation, 21
  enhancing, 21
  problem definition, 21
  walkthroughs, 21
Pseudocode:
  CASE logic, 145
  defined, 136
  DISPERR subroutine, 144
  false condition, assumed action of, 139
  and flowcharts, 138, 139
  GOTO statement, 142
  idiot checks, 143, 145
  indentation, 139, 141-42
  in IPO diagrams, 145-46
  INPTRX, subroutine, 141, 142
  jumps, 142, 143
  key words in, 137
  loop types, 140
  nesting, 143
Psychology of Computer Programming, The, 177

S

Safety. *See* Integrity
Sequential access method, 158-60
  characteristics, 160
  deletions, 160
  discussion, 158-59
  example, 159
Shared processing step, 61
Shared processing symbols, use, 62

Structural diagram:
  components, 47
  control flow, 47-49
  descriptive words, 53-54, 56
  detail, degrees of, 49-53
    discussion, 49, 52-53
    going to work, example, 50-51
  expansion, 49
  going to work, example, 48
  "KISS" rule, 53
  processing control from main function, 48
  and subfunctions, 48
Structural diagram development, review of:
  communication between users and programmers, 66
  questions to ask self, 64, 65
  summary, 66-67
  and use by people, 65
Structured Walkthroughs, 177-78
Subroutines, 61, 124-26
  discussion, 124
  DISPERR, calls for, 125
  display symbol, 126
  flowchart for, 127
Symbols, special, 62
Synthesizers, 16
Systems, computer, defined, 6

T

Tables, 150-52
  employee information arrays, 152
  one-dimensional, 151
  subscripts, 151
  two-dimensional, 151
Testing:
  amount of, 186
  attitudes, personal, 196
  debugging, 184, 185
  display screens, 193-94
  documentation, 191
  error avalanche, 186
  HIPOs, 192
  logic-path, 192
  in machines, 185
  nature of, 184

normal values, 192
objectives:
  integration, 189
  reliability, 188-89
organization, 189-91
  bottom-up, 190-91
  and dummy modules, 190
  evolutionary, 190
  overconfident approach, 189-90
  top-down, 190
overview of, 186-88
  assistance, 187
  attitudes, 187
  as demolition derby, 187
  educational aspect, 187-88
  tasks, 188
performing of, 194-96
plans, "goodness" of, 191
post-handling, 194-95
preparation for, 191-94
  discussion, 191-92
reliability, evaluation of, 185-86
resource limitation, 186
session documentation form, 195
software vs. hardware, 196
tabular specification of, 193
test files, 192

V

Variables, defined, 149
Verbs, module description:
  general, 55
  input, 54
  output, 55
  processor, 54-55
VTOC. *See* HIPOs

W

Weinberg, Gerald, 177

Y

Yourdan, Edward, 177